Academic
Learning
Series

Microsoft®
Windows NT®
Technical
Support

Lab Manual

Microsoft *Press*

PUBLISHED BY
Microsoft Press
A Division of Microsoft Corporation
One Microsoft Way
Redmond, Washington 98052-6399

Library of Congress Cataloging-in-Publication Data
Microsoft Windows NT Technical Support: Academic Learning Series / Microsoft Corporation
     p.   cm.
  Includes index.
  ISBN 1-57231-373-0
  ISBN 1-57231-911-9 (Academic Learning Series)
  1. Microsoft Windows NT.   2. Operating systems (Computers)
I. Microsoft Corporation.
QA76.76.063M52435   1997
005.74--DC21   97-830
                                              CIP

Printed and bound in the United States of America.

5 6 7 8 9 WCWC 3 2 1 0 9

Distributed in Canada by ITP Nelson, a division of Thomson Canada Limited.

A CIP catalogue record for this book is available from the British Library.

Microsoft Press books are available through booksellers and distributors worldwide. For further
information about international editions, contact your local Microsoft Corporation office, or
contact Microsoft Press International directly at fax (425) 936-7329. Visit our Web site at
mspress.microsoft.com.

Acquisitions Editor: William Setten
Series Editor: Barbara Moreland

Part No. 097-0002053

Introduction to Lab Exercises

Included with the Academic Learning Series (ALS) texts are hands-on lab exercises designed to give you practical experience using Microsoft Windows NT 4.0. This hands-on experience is an essential part of your training because it is difficult to truly understand and use the operating system and its features without having had the opportunity to explore firsthand the menus, options, and responses. The tasks included in these exercises provide an opportunity for you to test the concepts presented in the text, to use Microsoft Windows NT's utilities and tools, and to explore the structure of Microsoft Windows NT's operating system.

The lab exercises are best used in a classroom setting, though some exercises can be completed individually. The exercises presume a classroom network setup in one or more Windows NT domains with shared resources (depending upon the specific ALS text being used).

The directory of subdirectories, programs, and data files designed to support these labs can be shared from the instructor's system or installed on each student's system. A lab setup guide is provided for the instructor to use in setting up the classroom to support the labs.

The lab exercises do not precisely mirror the text's practice activities. Domain names, user names, IP addresses, shared resources, and other specific references in the lab exercises may be somewhat different from similar references in the ALS text or from those used in setting up the classroom network.

Local constraints must be followed to ensure proper network operations. Since it is not possible to predict each institution's local networking requirements, your instructor will explain differences that occur.

The old saying "The way to get to Carnegie Hall is to practice, practice, practice" is equally true of the pursuit of personal competency and Microsoft Certification. The tests required for Microsoft Certified Product Specialist, Systems Engineer, or other Microsoft certifications are demanding. One of the best ways to become confident in the use of Microsoft Windows NT is to complete each of the assigned lab exercises as well as the practice tasks included in the text.

Lab 1: Installing and Exploring Windows NT Server

Objectives

After completing this lab, you will be able to:

- Install Microsoft Windows NT Server version 4.0.
- Configure Windows NT Books Online.

Before You Begin

You will need the following to complete this lab:

- Three blank disks to be used for creating the Setup disks.
- One blank disk to be used for creating an Emergency Repair Disk.
- Your assigned student number, x. Substitute this number when you encounter a lowercase, italic x throughout all labs. For example, if you are assigned number 3, whenever you see Server$x$ in the labs, substitute Server3.
- Appropriate configuration settings for your network adapter card, if they are not the default values.

Your computer is configured as shown in the following table.

Partition type	Option	Drive C	Drive D	Drive E	Free space
Primary	Minimum partition size	15 MB			
Extended	Minimum partition size (all remaining)		200 MB	175 MB	100 MB
	Active partition	Yes	No	No	N/A
	Current operating system	MS-DOS	N/A	N/A	N/A
	File system	FAT	FAT	FAT	N/A

You will keep Microsoft Windows NT Workstation on drive E and install Windows NT Server on drive D.

Estimated time to complete this lab: 75 minutes

Exercise 1
Installing Windows NT Server Over the Network

In this exercise, you will install Windows NT Server 4.0 onto your computer over the network, creating the three Windows NT Server boot disks and an Emergency Repair Disk.

➤ **To copy the Windows NT Server files from the network**

1. Press CTRL+ALT+DEL, and then click **Logoff**.

2. Click **OK** to log off.

3. Log on to the CLASSROOM domain as Administrator, using the password **password**

4. Click the **Start** button, and then click **Run**.

5. In the **Open** box, type **\\Instructor\Ntsrv\winnt32** and then click **OK**.

6. Setup prompts you for the location of the Windows NT files.

7. To accept the default path of \\Instructor\Ntsrv, click **Continue**.

8. When prompted, label a blank disk as *Windows NT Server Setup Disk #3*, insert it in drive A, and then click **OK**. When prompted, label a blank disk as *Windows NT Server Setup Disk #2*, insert it into drive A, and then click **OK**.

9. When prompted, label a blank disk as *Windows NT Server Setup Boot Disk*, insert it into drive A, and then click **OK**.

   While Winnt32.exe copies files to the three setup disks, another thread of Winnt32.exe copies files to a temporary directory on the hard disk.

➤ **To complete the initializing installation phase of Windows NT Server Setup**

1. Leave the Windows NT Server Setup Boot Disk in drive A.

2. Click Restart Computer to restart the computer.

3. When prompted, insert Windows NT Server Setup Disk #2 in drive A, and then press enter.

4. Read the Welcome to Setup screen, and then press enter to continue.

5. Press enter to have Windows NT Setup automatically detect mass storage devices.

6. When prompted, insert Windows NT Server Setup Disk #3 in drive A, and then press enter.

7. When prompted, press enter to confirm the detected devices.

8. When the Windows NT End User License Agreement dialog box appears, press PAGE DOWN to scroll through it and read it.

9. Press F8 to accept the terms of the agreement.

10. When prompted, press N to cancel the upgrade of Windows NT Workstation and to install a fresh copy of Windows NT.

11. Press ENTER to confirm the detected hardware and software components.

12. Select drive D, and then press ENTER to install Windows NT Server on drive D.

13. Select **Leave the current file system intact (no changes)**, and then press ENTER.

14. Press ENTER to confirm the default installation directory of \WINNT.

15. Press ENTER to have Setup examine your hard disk.

    Setup copies files to the hard disk. This process may take a few minutes.

16. When prompted, remove the disk from drive A, and then press ENTER to restart your computer.

➤ **To complete the gathering-information phase of Windows NT Setup**

After your computer has restarted, the Windows NT Server Setup wizard appears.

1. Click **Next** to begin gathering information about your computer.

   Windows NT Setup creates the folder hierarchy for your installation.

2. Type your name and organization, and then click **Next**.

3. Type **040-0048126** for your CD key, and then click **Next**.

4. Click **Per Server**, enter **30** concurrent connections, and then click **Next**.

5. In the **Name** box, type **Server**x (where x is your assigned student number), and then click **Next**.

6. Click Primary Domain Controller, and then click Next.

7. In the **Password** and **Confirm Password** boxes, type **password** for the Administrator account password, and then click **Next**.

8. If you see a message indicating that your computer exhibits a floating-point divide problem, click **Do not enable the floating-point workaround**, and then click **Next**.

9. Click Yes, create an emergency repair disk (recommended), and then click Next.

10. Click **Next** to accept the default components.

➤ **To complete the installing networking phase of Windows NT Server Setup**

1. Click **Next** to begin installing Windows NT Networking.

2. Click **Next** to confirm that your computer is wired to the network.

3. Click to clear the **Install Microsoft Internet Information Server** check box, and then click **Next** to skip installation of IIS.

4. Click **Start Search** to have Windows NT Server Setup detect your network adapter.

5. Unless your instructor tells you otherwise, click **Next** to confirm the detected network adapter.

6. Click to clear the **NWLink IPX/SPX Compatible Transport** check box, verify that the **TCP/IP Protocol** check box is the only one selected, and then click **Next**.

7. Click **Next** to confirm the selected network services.

8. Click **Next** to install the selected network components.

9. If told to do so by your instructor, enter the appropriate configuration settings for your network adapter, and then click **Continue** to confirm the settings.

10. Click **Yes** to use DHCP.

    Windows NT Server Setup installs and then configures the networking components.

11. Click **Next** to accept the default bindings.

12. Click **Next** to start the network.

13. In the **Domain** box, type **Domain***x* (where *x* is your assigned student number), and then click **Next** to create the domain.

➤ **To complete the finishing phase of Windows NT Server Setup**

1. Click Finish to begin finishing setup.

2. In the Time Zone list, select the time zone for your location, confirm that the Date and **Time** options are correct, and then click **Close**.

3. Click **OK** to confirm the detected video adapter.

4. Click **Test** to test the settings for your video adapter, and then click **OK**.

5. If you did not see the test bitmap, adjust your settings and test again. If you did see the test bitmap, click **Yes**, and then click **OK**.

6. Click **OK** to confirm the video settings.

   Windows NT Server Setup copies additional files to the hard disk, removes temporary files, and saves the configuration to the emergency repair directory.

7. When prompted, label a blank disk as *Emergency Repair Disk*, insert it into drive A, and then click **OK**.

   Windows NT formats the disk and then copies the emergency repair information.

8. When prompted, remove the Emergency Repair Disk from drive A, and then click **Restart Computer**.

   The computer is restarted, and then you are given the option to select an operating system.

9. Select Windows NT Server version 4.00.

Exercise 2
Configuring and Using Windows NT Books Online

In this exercise, you will configure your copy of Windows NT Server Books Online to obtain the documentation from a shared resource on the Instructor computer. You will then use this resource.

➤ **To use Books Online**

1. Log on as Administrator, using the password **password**

2. Click the **Start** button, point to **Programs**, and then click **Books Online**.

3. In the **Location of Books Online Files** box, type **\\Instructor\Books** and then click **OK**.

4. The **Help Topics: Windows NT 4.0 Books Online** dialog box appears.

5. Double-click **Microsoft Windows NT Server Books Online**.

6. Double-click **Concepts and Planning**.

7. Double-click **Managing Windows NT Server Domains**.

8. Double-click **Directory Services and Domains**, the second entry under **Managing Windows NT Server Domains**.

9. After reading the text, exit Books Online.

Exercise 3
Installing Course Materials

In this exercise, you will install course materials that will be used throughout the course. The course materials include lab files and a shortcut to Microsoft Windows NT 4.0 Technical Support, which contains appendixes, simulations, and supplemental materials. You will also install Microsoft Internet Explorer 3.0 on your computer running Windows NT Server.

➤ **To install course materials**

1. Right-click the My Computer icon, and then click **Map Network Drive**.

2. Map drive M to \\Instructor\CourseCD.

3. On drive M, run the Setup program.

   The **Microsoft Windows NT 4.0 Technical Support** dialog box appears.

4. Click **Continue**.

5. Click **Student Computer Setup**.

   The required course files are copied to and installed on the hard disk.

6. Click **OK**.

➤ **To install Microsoft Internet Explorer 3.0**

1. On drive M, open the IE_Setup folder, and then run the Msie30 program.

   A **Microsoft Internet Explorer 3.0** dialog box appears, prompting for confirmation to install Microsoft Internet Explorer 3.0.

2. Click **Yes** to install Microsoft Internet Explorer 3.0.

   A **Microsoft Internet Explorer Setup** dialog box appears, indicating that files are being copied to a temporary folder on your hard disk.

3. Read the End-User License Agreement for Microsoft Internet Explorer, and then click **I Agree** to accept the terms of the agreement and to continue the installation.

   A **Microsoft Internet Explorer Setup** dialog box appears, indicating that files are being copied and Microsoft Internet Explorer is being set up on your computer.

4. When prompted to restart your computer, click **Yes**.

Lab 2: Adding Computers to a Domain

Objectives

After completing this lab, you will be able to add a computer running Windows NT Workstation, or a member server running Windows NT Server, to a domain.

Before You Begin

You will work with another student in this lab. One student will perform Exercise 1, where the computer will join the domain by supplying domain administrator creden-tials at the time it joins the domain (referred to as workstation A in Exercise 1). The other student will perform Exercise 2, where the computer will join the domain when the computer account already exists in the domain (referred to as workstation B in Exercise 2).

Determine which student will perform Exercise 1 and which student will perform Exercise 2. If you will be performing Exercise 2, tell the instructor which computer account to create on the PDC for the CLASSROOM domain.

Estimated time to complete this lab: 10 minutes

Exercise 1
Joining a Domain by Supplying Administrator Credentials

In this exercise, you will add your computer running Windows NT Workstation to the CLASSROOM domain. This exercise requires you to supply a valid domain administrator's user name and password when you join the domain.

Perform this exercise at workstation A.

➤ **To join the domain by supplying administrator credentials (at workstation A)**

1. Log on as Administrator, using the password **password**

2. In Control Panel, double-click the Network icon.

3. On the **Identification** tab, click **Change**.

   The **Identification Changes** dialog box appears.

4. Click **Domain**.

5. In the **Domain** box, type **CLASSROOM**

6. Click to select the **Create a Computer Account in the Domain** check box.

7. In the **User Name** box, type **ClassAdmin**

8. In the **Password** box, type **classpass** and then click **OK**.

   A **Network Configuration** dialog box appears, welcoming you to the CLASSROOM domain.

9. Click **OK**.

10. In the **Network** dialog box, click **Close**.

    A **Network Settings Change** dialog box appears, indicating that you need to restart the computer.

11. Click **Yes**.

12. Wait until your computer has restarted.

    The **Begin Logon** dialog box appears.

13. Press CTRL+ALT+DELETE.

14. In the **User name** box, type **ClassAdmin**

15. In the **Password** box, type **classpass**

16. To log on to the domain, in the **Domain** box, click **CLASSROOM**, and then click **OK**.

Exercise 2
Joining a Domain When the Computer Account Already Exists

In this exercise, you will add your computer running Windows NT Workstation to the CLASSROOM domain when the computer account already exists on the PDC and therefore does not require you to supply domain administrator credentials.

Perform this exercise at workstation B.

➤ **To join the domain when the computer account already exists (at workstation B)**

1. Log on as Administrator, using the password **password**

2. In Control Panel, double-click the Network icon.

3. On the Identification tab, click Change.

   The **Identification Changes** dialog box appears.

4. Click **Domain**.

5. In the **Domain** box, type **CLASSROOM**

Important   Before proceeding, ensure your instructor has created an account for your computer and tells you to proceed.

---

1. Click **OK**.

   A **Network Configuration** dialog box appears, welcoming you to the CLASSROOM domain.

2. Click **OK**.

3. In the **Network** dialog box, click **Close**.

   A **Network Settings Change** dialog box appears, indicating that you need to restart the computer.

4. Click **Yes**.

5. Wait until your computer has restarted.

   The **Begin Logon** dialog box appears.

6. Press CTRL + ALT + DELETE.

7. In the User name box, type ClassAdmin

8. In the **Password** box, type **classpass**

9. To log on to the domain, in the **Domain** box, click **CLASSROOM**, and then click **OK**.

Lab 3: Creating a Network Installation Startup Disk *(optional)*

Objective

After completing this lab, you will be able to:

■ Create and use a network installation startup disk.

Before You Begin

This lab requires that you have a floppy disk that has been formatted as an MS-DOS system disk.

You will need to know what kind of network adapter you have. If you do not know this information, please ask the instructor.

You will need to supply a unique computer name. If you are not sure what to use, please ask the instructor.

Estimated time to complete this lab: 20 minutes

Exercise 1
Creating an Over-the-Network Installation Disk

In this exercise, you will create an over-the-network installation disk.

Note Complete this exercise on your computer running Windows NT Server.

➤ **To create an over-the-network installation disk**

1. Click the Start button, point to Programs, point to Administrative Tools (Common), and then click Network Client Administrator.

2. In the **Network Client Administrator** dialog box, verify that **Make Network Installation Startup Disk** is selected, and then click **Continue**.

   The **Share Network Client Installation Files** dialog box appears.

3. Click **Use existing path**, type **\\Instructor\Clients** in the **Path** box, and then click **OK**.

   The **Target Workstation Configuration** dialog box appears.

4. Under **Floppy Drive**, click the correct size of drive A.

5. In the **Network Adapter Card** box, click the correct network adapter card, and then click **OK**.

   The **Network Startup Disk Configuration** dialog box appears.

6. In the **Computer Name** box, type a unique computer name, and then click **OK**.

   The **Network Client Administrator** dialog box appears.

7. Insert a blank, formatted 1.44-MB MS-DOS system disk into drive A, and then click **OK**.

   The **Confirm Network Disk Configuration** dialog box appears, asking you to verify the information.

8. Click **OK.**

   A **Network Client Administrator** dialog box appears, indicating that all of the files have been successfully copied to the disk.

9. Click **OK**.

10. Click **Exit** to close Network Client Administrator.

A **Network Client Administrator** dialog box, displaying the following check list, appears:

```
Make sure you have sufficient permissions to access this shared
directory.
Be sure to enter a unique computer name on startup disk for each
machine being configured over the network.
The network adapter card was configured using default settings.
Verify the settings and modify them if necessary.
```

11. Click **OK**.

12. Shut down your computer, and then restart your computer using the network installation startup disk that you created.

13. Connect to \\Instructor\Clients.

Were you successful?

_____

14. Remove the network installation startup disk from drive A, and then restart the computer as Windows NT Server.

Lab 4: Using the Registry Editor

Objective

After completing this lab, you will be able to:

- View and find information in the registry by using Regedt32.exe.

Before You Begin

In the Administrative Tools folder, create a shortcut for the Registry Editor (D:\Winnt\System32\Regedt32.exe). This will provide quick access to Registry Editor.

Estimated time to complete this lab: 25 minutes

Exercise 1
Exploring the Registry

In this exercise, you will use the Registry Editor to view information in the registry.

Note Complete this exercise on your computer running Windows NT Server.

➤ **To locate information in the registry**

1. Verify that you are logged on as Administrator.

2. Start Registry Editor (Regedt32.exe).

3. On the **Options** menu, click to select **Read Only Mode**.

   There should now be a check mark by **Read Only Mode**, indicating that it is selected.

4. On the **View** menu, verify that **Tree and Data** is selected.

5. Minimize all windows except HKEY_LOCAL_MACHINE on Local Machine.

6. Expand the **HARDWARE\DESCRIPTION\System** subkey and locate the information requested in the second table, using the subkeys under the **System** key. The first table is an example.

Hardware configuration	System subkeys	Value and string
Processor type (example)	**CentralProcessor\0**	**Identifier:80486**
Bus type (example)	**MultifunctionAdapter\0**	**Identifier:ISA**
Pointer controller type (example)	**MultifunctionAdapter\0\ PointerController\0\ PointerPeripheral\0**	**Identifier:MICROSOFT PS2 MOUSE**
Pointer controller type (EISA example)	**EisaAdapter\0\ PointerController\0\ PointerPeripheral\0**	**Identifier:MICROSOFT PS2 MOUSE**

Hardware configuration	System subkeys	Value and string
Processor type		
Bus type		
Pointer controller type		

7. Expand the SOFTWARE\Microsoft\Windows NT\Current Version subkey, and then locate the following information:

Software configuration	Value and string
Registered owner	
Registered organization	
Current version	
Current build number	

➤ **To use the Find Key command**

1. Select the **HKEY_LOCAL_MACHINE** subkey located at the top of the path. This will ensure that the entire subtree will be searched.

2. On the **View** menu, click **Find Key**.

3. In the **Find What** box, type **serial** and then click **Find Next**.

4. Click **Find Next** until a **Warning** dialog box appears, stating that Registry Editor cannot find the desired key.

    Notice that this key appears in multiple locations in the registry.

5. Click **OK** to close the **Warning** dialog box.

6. In the **Find** dialog box, click **Cancel** to end the search.

➤ **To view a configuration change in the registry**

1. In Control Panel, double-click the System icon.

2. In the **System Properties** dialog box, click the **Environment** tab.

3. In the **System Variables** box, click any variable.

    The focus is now set on the **System Variables** box.

4. In the **Variable** box, type **TEST**

5. In the **Value** box, type **Yes** and then click **Set**.

6. Click **OK**.

7. Switch to Registry Editor.

    Does the **TEST** variable appear in **HKEY_LOCAL_MACHINE\SYSTEM\CurrentControlSet\Control\ Session Manager\Environment**?

8. Close Control Panel.

➤   **To search a subtree for a specific value**

1. Click HKEY_LOCAL_MACHINE\SOFTWARE.

2. On the Registry menu, click Save Subtree As.

3. Save the file to your desktop with the name Software.txt

4. Close Registry Editor.

5. On your desktop, double-click the text file called Software.

    Notepad opens the Software.txt file.

6. On the Search menu, click Find.

7. In the Find What box, type CurrentBuildNumber and then click Find Next.

8. Click Cancel to close the Find dialog box.

9. Scroll down (if necessary) to see the data for CurrentBuildNumber.

    What is this value's data?

    _____

10. Close Notepad.

Lab 5: Using Control Panel

Objectives

After completing this lab, you will be able to:

- Create and select a network-disabled hardware profile.
- Configure the boot delay.
- Change the paging file size.
- Install optional Windows NT components.

Before You Begin

On your desktop, create a shortcut to Control Panel for quick and easy access to the Control Panel programs.

Prerequisite

Lab 2: Adding Computers to a Domain.

Estimated time to complete this lab: 25 minutes

Exercise 1
Managing Hardware Profiles

In this exercise, you will use the System program to create a network-disabled hardware profile for Windows NT Workstation.

Note   Complete this exercise on your computer running Windows NT Workstation.

➤ **To create a network-disabled hardware profile for Windows NT Workstation**

1. Shut down and restart your computer as Windows NT Workstation.

2. Log on to the CLASSROOM domain as Administrator.

3. In Control Panel, double-click the System icon.

4. Click the **Hardware Profiles** tab.

5. Click **Rename**.

   The **Rename Profile** dialog box appears.

6. In the **To** box, type **On the Network** and then click **OK**.

7. Click **Copy**.

   The **Copy Profile** dialog box appears.

8. In the **To** box, type **Off the Network** and then click **OK**.

9. Click **Off the Network**, and then click **Properties**.

10. Click the **Network** tab.

11. Click to select the **Network-disabled hardware profile** check box, and then click **OK**.

12. Under **Multiple Hardware Profiles,** in the **Wait for user selection for** box, change the value to **10** seconds.

13. Click **OK**.

➤ **To choose a hardware profile during system boot**

1. Shut down and restart Windows NT Workstation.

2. On the **Hardware Profile/Configuration Recovery** menu, click **Off the Network**, and then press ENTER.

3. Log on to the CLASSROOM domain as Administrator.

   What message appears?

   Classroom not available

   Why does this message appear?

   _____

4. Click **OK** to close the **Logon Message** dialog box.

5. Shut down Windows NT Workstation, and then restart Windows NT Server.

Exercise 2
Decreasing the Boot Delay

In this exercise, you will decrease the boot delay by changing the number of seconds of delay before the default operating system is loaded.

Note Complete this exercise on your computer running Windows NT Server.

➤ **To decrease the boot delay**

1. Shut down, and then restart Windows NT Server to observe the number of seconds that it takes for Windows NT Server to load.

2. Log on as Administrator.

3. In Control Panel, double-click the System icon.

4. Click the **Startup/Shutdown** tab.

5. In the **Show list for** box, set the number of seconds to **5**, and then click **OK**.

6. Shut down and restart Windows NT Server to see the results of decreasing the boot delay setting.

Exercise 3
Changing the Paging File Size

In this exercise, you will use the System program to change the size of the Windows NT paging file.

Note Complete this exercise on your computer running Windows NT Server.

➤ **To change the paging file size**

1. Log on as Administrator.

2. In Control Panel, double-click the System icon.

3. Click the **Performance** tab.

4. Click **Change**.

   The **Virtual Memory** dialog box appears.

5. In the **Drive** box, click the drive that contains your paging file.

6. In the **Initial Size** box, increase the value by 10, and then click **Set**.

   If you do not click **Set**, the change will not occur.

7. If you receive a System Control Panel Applet indicating that the drive does not have enough free space for the maximum paging file specified, click **OK**.

8. Click **OK**.

9. Click **Close**.

   The **System Settings Change** dialog box appears.

10. Click **Yes** to shut down and restart Windows NT Server.

11. After Windows NT Server restarts, log on as Administrator and confirm the new settings by using the System program in Control Panel.

Exercise 4
Installing Optional Windows NT Components

In this exercise, you will use Add/Remove Programs to install the Windows NT games.

Note Complete this exercise on your computer running Windows NT Server.

➤ **To add additional Windows NT components**

1. In Control Panel, double-click the Add/Remove Programs icon.

2. Click the **Windows NT Setup** tab.

3. Click to select the **Games** check box, and then click **OK**.

    The **Files Needed** dialog box appears.

Lab 6: Implementing System Policies

Objective

After completing this lab, you will be able to:

- Create and implement a system policy for a domain computer.

Before You Begin

To complete this lab, you must work with a partner. One computer will be running Windows NT Server, and will be used to configure a system policy for the domain. The other computer, running Windows NT Workstation, will be migrated to the DOMAINx domain (where x is the assigned student number for the computer running Windows NT Server), and will then be used to test the system policy. Decide now who will play each role. At the end of the lab, you will reverse roles and complete the lab again.

You will need your partner's assigned student number to complete this lab:

Prerequisite

Lab 2: Adding Computers to a Domain.

Estimated time to complete this lab: 20 minutes

Exercise 1
Implementing System Policies

In this exercise, you will create and implement a system policy for a computer running Windows NT Workstation. The system policy will be implemented at the computer that will be the PDC for a domain consisting of one Windows NT Server and one Windows NT Workstation computer.

Note Complete this exercise on the computer running Windows NT Server.

➤ **To create a system policy for a computer running Windows NT Workstation**

1. Click the Start button, point to Programs, point to Administrative Tools (Common), and then click System Policy Editor.

2. On the **File** menu, click **New Policy**.

3. On the **Edit** menu, click **Add Computer**.

4. In the **Add Computer** dialog box, type **Workstation**x (where x is your partner's assigned student number), and then click **OK**.

5. Double-click the Workstationx icon.

   The **Workstation**x **Properties** dialog box appears.

6. Expand **Windows NT System**.

7. Expand **Logon**.

8. Click to select the **Logon Banner** check box.

9. In the **Caption** box, type **Attention**

10. In the **Text** box, type **Unauthorized use of Workstation**x **is prohibited**

11. Click to select the **Enable shutdown from Authentication dialog box** check box, and then click it once again to clear the check box.

12. Click to select the **Do not display last logged on user name** check box, and then click **OK**.

13. On the **File** menu, click **Save**.

14. Save the file in the D:\Winnt\System32\Repl\Import\Scripts folder, and name it **Ntconfig** (System Policy Editor will automatically append the .pol extension).

15. Exit System Policy Editor.

Exercise 2
Testing System Policies

In this exercise, you will restart one of the computers as a computer running Windows NT Workstation, migrate your computer running Windows NT Workstation from the CLASSROOM domain to your partner's domain, and then test the system policy for your computer running Windows NT Workstation.

Note Complete this exercise on the computer running Windows NT Workstation.

➤ **To migrate to another domain**

1. Shut down your computer, and then restart it as Windows NT Workstation.

2. Log on to the CLASSROOM domain as Administrator.

3. In Control Panel, double-click the Network icon.

4. Click the **Identification tab**, and then click **Change**.

5. In the **Domain** box, type **Domain**x (where x is your partner's assigned student number).

6. Click to select the **Create a computer account in the domain** check box.

7. In the **User Name** box, type **Domain**x**Administrator** (where x is your partner's assigned student number).

8. In the **Password** box, type **password** and then click **OK**.

9. Click **Yes** to move this computer out of the CLASSROOM domain.

10. Click **OK** to acknowledge the Welcome message.

11. Click **Close** to exit the Network program.

12. Click **Yes** to restart your computer, and then restart it as Windows NT Workstation.

➤ **To test the system policy**

1. Press CTRL+ALT+DELETE to log on.

   Are the policy settings in effect? Why or why not?

   YES.

2. Finish logging on to DOMAIN*x* as Administrator, and then log off.

3. Press CTRL+ALT+DELETE to log on.

   Are the policy settings in effect? Why or why not?

   YES

4. Finish logging on to DOMAIN*x* as Administrator.

5. Shut down your computer, and then restart it as Windows NT Server.

6. Log on as Administrator.

Exercise 3 *(optional)*
Reversing Roles

In this exercise, you will reverse roles, and repeat Exercises 1 and 2.

➤ **To reverse roles**

1. If your computer was the computer running Windows NT Workstation in Exercise 2, perform Exercise 1 now.

2. If your computer was the computer running Windows NT Server in Exercise 1, wait until your partner has completed Exercise 1, and then perform Exercise 2.

Lab 7: Converting a FAT Partition to NTFS

Objective

After completing this lab, you will be able to:

- Convert a file allocation table (FAT) partition to Windows NT File System (NTFS).

Estimated time to complete this lab: 10 minutes

Exercise 1
Converting a FAT Partition to NTFS

In this exercise, you will convert your Windows NT Server boot partition to NTFS.

Note Complete this exercise on your computer running Windows NT Server.

➤ **To convert from FAT to NTFS**

1. Click the **Start** button, point to **Program**s, and then click **Command Prompt**.

2. In the Command Prompt window, type **convert d: /fs:ntfs** and then press ENTER.

   A message appears, stating that **convert** cannot gain exclusive access to drive D and cannot convert it now.

   Why does this message occur?

   _____

3. Type **y** and then press ENTER to schedule the conversion for the next time the system is restarted.

4. Shut down and restart the computer as Windows NT Server.

   The conversion process occurs.

Note The system will restart itself a second time. Make sure you start your computer as Windows NT Server.

---

5. After the computer has restarted, log on as Administrator.

6. Right-click the My Computer icon, and then click **Explore**.

   Windows NT Explorer appears.

7. Right-click **drive D**, and then click **Properties**.

   What file system is on drive D?

   _____NTFS_____

8. Click **Cancel**.

9. Close Windows NT Explorer.

Lab 8: Managing Long File Names

Objective

After completing this lab, you will be able to:

- Create and manage files with long file names.

Before You Begin

Before starting the exercises, make sure that Windows NT Explorer is configured to hide file extensions for known file types. This is a default setting. If the setting is changed, the exercises in this lab will not work as written.

Estimated time to complete this lab: 15 minutes

Exercise 1
Managing Long File Names

In this exercise, you will create and rename files, and then note the effect of these changes on their long file names and aliases. Make sure you type the names exactly as specified, including capitalization and spacing.

Note Complete this exercise on your computer running Windows NT Server.

➤ **To create long file names**

1. Right-click the My Computer icon, and then click **Explore**.

   Windows NT Explorer appears.

2. In Windows NT Explorer, click the icon for drive C.

3. On the **File** menu, point to **New**, and then click **Folder** to create a new folder.

4. Name the folder *LFN Lab Exercise*

5. Use Windows NT Explorer to create the following text documents in the LFN Lab Exercise folder:

   Long filename.lab.exercise

   Long filename.exercise.lab

   Longfilename.exercise.lab

   Exercise.long filename.lab

   Lab.long filename.exercise

   Test.Txt

6. Start a Command Prompt, and then change to the root directory of drive C (C:\).

7. Type **dir /x** and then press ENTER to list the root directory.

   How does the folder that you just created appear in the directory list?

   <u>LNFLAB~1   LNF Lab Exsreiss</u>

8. Type **cd lfn lab exercise** and then press ENTER to change to the directory you created.

9. Type **dir /x** and then press ENTER to list the directory contents. Record the 8.3 file names in the following table.

8.3 file names	Long file names
Longfi~1.txt	Long filename.lab.exercise.txt
	Long filename.exercise.lab.txt
	Longfilename.exercise.lab.txt
	Exercise.long filename.lab.txt
	Lab.long filename.exercise.txt
	Test.Txt.txt

Why does Test.Txt have two extensions when listed from the Command Prompt window?

_____

10. Type **ren LONGFI~1.TXT LFN.LAB** and then press ENTER to rename LONGFI~1.TXT to LFN.LAB.

11. List the directory contents and note the file name and alias.

What happened to the file name and alias of the file you renamed?

_____

12. Type **ren "long filename.exercise.lab.txt" LONG.TXT** and then press ENTER.

Be sure to use quotation marks around the long file name because the **ren** command does not recognize blank spaces.

13. List the directory contents.

What happened to the file name and alias of the file you renamed?

_____

14. Type **ren LONG.TXT Long.Txt** and then press ENTER.

15. List the directory contents.

What happened to the file name and alias of the file you renamed?

_____

Why does Long.Txt have an alias while LONG.TXT does not?

_____

16. Close the Command Prompt window.

17. Close Windows NT Explorer.

Lab 9: Managing NTFS Compression

Objectives

After completing this lab, you will be able to:

Compress and decompress folders on an NTFS partition.

Manage compressed files on an NTFS partition.

Before You Begin

Prerequisite

Lab 7: Converting a FAT Partition to NTFS.

Estimated time to complete this lab: 20 minutes

Exercise 1
Compressing Files in an NTFS Partition

In this exercise, you will use Windows NT Explorer to compress files and folders to make more disk space available on your NTFS partition.

Note   Complete this exercise on your computer running Windows NT Server.

➤ **To compress a directory**

1. Right-click the My Computer icon, and then click **Explore**.

2. Examine the properties for drive D.

   What is the capacity of drive D?

   1.99 G

   What is the free space on drive D?

   1.73 G

3. Click to select the **Compress D:** check box, and then click **Apply**.

   A **Windows NT Explorer** dialog box appears.

4. Click to select the **Also compress subfolders** check box, and then click **OK**.

   A **Windows NT Explorer** dialog box appears, stating that Windows NT Explorer cannot change the compress attributes for D:\Pagefile.sys.

5. Click **Ignore All** to continue.

   A **Compress Files Progress** dialog box appears, indicating the progress of the compression. Compression may take several minutes.

   How much free space is available on drive D after compression?

   1.78 G

6. Click **OK** to close the **Properties** dialog box.

➤ **To display compressed files and folders with an alternate color**

1. In Windows NT Explorer, on the **View** menu, click **Options**.

2. On the View tab, click to select the Display compressed files and folders with alternate color check box.

3. Click **OK**.

   The compressed files and folders are displayed in blue.

➤ **To uncompress a folder**

1. In Windows NT Explorer, expand the icon for drive D.

2. Expand the LabFiles folder, expand the Ntfs folder, and then expand the Student folder.

3. In the Student folder, right-click the Archives folder.

4. Click Properties.

5. Click to clear the **Compress** check box, and then click **OK**.

6. A **Windows NT Explorer** dialog box appears.

7. Click to select the **Also uncompress subfolders** check box, and then click **OK**.

   The Archives folder name should be displayed in black. If not, press F5 to refresh the display.

Exercise 2
Copying and Moving Files

In this exercise, you will see the effects that copying and moving files have on compressed files.

Note Complete this exercise on your computer running Windows NT Server.

➤ **To copy a compressed file to an decompressed folder**

1. Examine the properties for
   D:\LabFiles\Ntfs\Student\Reports\Statistics\Dna.txt.

   Is Dna.txt compressed or decompressed?

   _____Yes ✓_____

2. Copy Dna.txt to the D:\LabFiles\Ntfs\Student\Archives folder.

   Make sure you copy (hold down the CTRL key while you drag the file) and do not move the file.

3. Examine the properties for Dna.txt in the Archives folder.

   Is Dna.txt compressed or decompressed?

   _____No._____

   Why?

   _____

   _____

➤ **To move a compressed file to an decompressed folder**

1. Examine the properties of D:\LabFiles\Ntfs\Student\Reports\Tech\Labor.txt.

   Is Labor.txt compressed or decompressed?

   _____Com_____

2. Move Labor.txt to the D:\LabFiles\Ntfs\Student\Archives folder.

3. Examine the properties for Labor.txt in the Archives folder.

   Is Labor.txt compressed or decompressed?

   _____Yes_____

   Why?

   _____

   _____

4. Close Windows NT Explorer.

Lab 10: Creating and Managing Partitions

Objectives

After completing this lab, you will be able to:

Create and manage partitions using Disk Administrator.

Create and manage a volume set.

Estimated time to complete this lab: 15 minutes

Exercise 1
Creating and Formatting Partitions

In this exercise, you will create a disk partition. Then you will format the partition and change the drive letter.

Note   Complete this exercise on your computer running Windows NT Server.

➤   **To create partitions**

1. Verify that you are logged on as Administrator.

2. Click the Start button, point to Programs, point to Administrative Tools (Common), and then click Disk Administrator.

Note   If this is the first time Disk Administrator has been run on your computer, the following will occur:

A **Disk Administrator** dialog box appears, stating that this is the first time that Disk Administrator has been run. Click **OK**.

A **Confirm** dialog box appears, stating that there is no signature found on Disk 0. Click **Yes**.

3. Maximize Disk Administrator.

What file systems are currently used on drives C, D, and E?

_____

_____

According to the information in the Disk Administrator window, how much free space does your computer have?

_____

_____

4. On the **Options** menu, click **Region Display**.

5. Under **Which disk**, click **All disks**.

6. Click **Size all regions equally**, and then click **OK**.

7. Select an area of free space on Disk 0, and then on the **Partition** menu, click **Create**.

A **Create Logical Drive** dialog box appears.

8. In the **Create logical drive of size** box, type **25** and then click **OK**.

The partition is created using the next available drive letter.

9. On the **Partition** menu, click **Commit Changes Now**.

   A **Confirm** dialog box appears, asking if you want to save the changes.

10. Click **Yes**.

    A **Disk Administrator** dialog box appears, stating that the disks were updated successfully.

11. Click **OK**.

➤ **To format a partition and label a volume**

1. Click the new unformatted partition, and then on the **Tools** menu, click **Format**.

2. In the **File System** box, click **NTFS**.

3. In the **Volume Label** box, type **ntfs-vol**

4. Click to select the **Quick Format** check box, and then click **Start**.

   A **Format** dialog box appears, warning that the operation will overwrite the data contained on this volume.

5. Click **OK**.

   A **Format Complete** dialog box appears.

6. Click **OK**.

7. Click **Close** to close the **Format** dialog box.

➤ **To change the drive letter**

1. Click the new formatted volume.

2. On the **Tools** menu, click **Assign Drive Letter**.

3. In the **Assign drive letter** box, click **I**, and then click **OK**.

   A **Confirm** dialog box appears, stating that the new drive letter assignment will happen immediately.

4. Click **Yes**.

Exercise 2
Extending an NTFS Partition

In this exercise, you will extend an NTFS partition.

Note Complete this exercise on your computer running Windows NT Server.

➤ **To extend an NTFS partition**

1. In Disk Administrator, click drive I, and while you hold down the ctrl key, click the remaining free space on Disk 0.

   Both areas should be selected.

2. On the **Partition** menu, click **Extend Volume S**et.

   An **Extend Volume Set** dialog box appears.

3. In the **Create volume set of total size** box, type **50** and then click **OK**.

   You have extended the NTFS volume. Notice that drive I appears in both region displays.

➤ **To exit and save changes**

1. On the **Partition** menu, click **Exit**.

2. Click **Yes** to confirm changes.

3. Click **Yes** to continue with the changes.

4. Click **OK** to acknowledge that the disks have been updated successfully.

5. Click **OK** to initiate system shutdown.

6. Restart your computer as Windows NT Server, and then log on as Administrator.

   Notice that **chkdsk** automatically runs as the computer reboots.

Exercise 3 *(optional)*
Creating and Managing a Volume Set

In this exercise, you will use a simulation to create, format, extend, and then delete a volume set. The Volume Set simulation will be used throughout this exercise to simulate Disk Administrator in a multiple-disk computer.

Note   Complete this exercise on your computer running Windows NT Server.

➤ **To start the simulation**

Click the **Start** button, point to **Programs**, point to **Microsoft Windows NT 4.0 Core Technologies Training**, point to **Simulations**, and then click **Volume Set Simulation**.

The simulation starts, and then Disk Administrator appears.

➤ **To create a volume set**

1. Click an area of free space on Disk 0.

   The area should now have a dark outline around it, indicating that it is selected.

2. Hold down the CTRL key, and click an area of free space on Disk 1.

   Both areas should now appear selected.

3. On the **Partition** menu, click **Create Volume Set**.

   The **Create Volume Set** dialog box appears. Notice in the **Create volume set of total size** box that the default is the actual total of the two areas of free space you selected.

4. Click **OK** to create a volume set of the maximum size possible on Disk 0 and Disk 1.

   The new volume set is created. Notice that the next available drive letter, G, has been assigned and that the color bar has changed. The new volume set is unformatted.

5. On the **Partition** menu, click **Commit Changes Now**.

   A **Confirm** message box appears, stating that changes have been made to your disk configuration.

6. Click **Yes** to save the changes.

   A **Confirm** dialog box appears, stating that the changes requested will require you to restart your computer.

7. Click **Yes** to continue with the changes.

A **Disk Administrator** dialog box appears, stating that the disks were updated successfully.

8. Click **OK**.

A **Disk Administrator** dialog box appears, stating that changes have been made that require you to restart your computer.

9. Click **OK** to initiate system shutdown.

A **Volume Set Simulation** dialog box appears, stating that the simulation will proceed as if a shutdown has occurred and you have logged on as Administrator.

10. Click **OK**.

A message box appears, prompting you to please wait while the system writes unsaved data to the disk.

The simulation continues with Disk Administrator open.

➤ **To format a volume set**

1. In Disk Administrator, click the unformatted volume set (drive G), and then on the **Tools** menu, click **Format**.

2. In the **File System** box, click **NTFS**, and then click **Start**.

3. Click **OK** to continue to format the volume set.

A **Formatting** dialog box appears, indicating that the format is complete.

4. Click **OK**.

5. Click **Close**.

The volume set now appears in Disk Administrator as an NTFS volume set.

➤ **To extend a volume set**

1. In Disk Administrator, click drive G, and then while holding down the ctrl key, click an area of free space on Disk 2.

All three areas should be selected.

2. On the **Partition** menu, click **Extend Volume Set**.

The **Extend Volume Set** dialog box appears. Notice in the **Create volume set of total size** box that the default is the maximum total size of the areas you selected.

3. Click **OK** to extend the volume set.

You have extended an existing NTFS volume. Notice that drive G appears in all three region displays for this volume set.

4. On the **Partition** menu, click **Exit**, and then click **Yes** to save your changes.

   A **Disk Administrator** dialog box appears, indicating that your disks were updated successfully.

5. Click **OK**.

   A **Disk Administrator** dialog box appears, indicating that the requested changes require you to restart your computer.

6. Click **OK** to restart your computer.

   A **Volume Set Simulation** dialog box appears, stating that the simulation will proceed as if a shutdown has occurred and you have logged on as Administrator.

7. Click **OK**.

   A dialog box appears, prompting you to please wait while the system writes unsaved data to the disk.

   The simulation continues with Disk Administrator open.

➤ **To delete a volume set**

1. In Disk Administrator, click drive G.

   All areas of drive G should now be selected.

2. On the **Partition** menu, click Delete.

   A **Confirm** dialog box appears, indicating that all data in the volume set will be lost.

3. Click **Yes** to delete the selected volume.

4. On the **Partition** menu, click Exit, and then click Yes to save your changes.

   A **Confirm** dialog box appears, indicating that the requested changes require you to restart your computer.

5. Click **Yes** to restart your computer.

   A **Disk Administrator** dialog box appears, indicating that the disks were updated successfully.

6. Click **OK**.

7. Click **OK** to initiate system shutdown.

   A **Volume Set Simulation** dialog box appears, indicating that this concludes the Volume Set Simulation exercise.

8. Click **OK**.

   Disk Administrator closes, and then the Volume Set simulation ends.

Lab 11: Implementing Fault Tolerance

Objectives

After completing this lab, you will be able to:

Implement disk striping with parity.

Implement disk mirroring.

Before You Begin

This lab uses the Implementing Fault Tolerance simulation, which simulates a computer with three hard disks. Alternatively, if your computer running Microsoft Windows NT Server has a minimum of three hard disks and available space for configuring the partitions, you may use Disk Administrator to complete the lab.

Estimated time to complete this lab: 10 minutes

Exercise 1
Using Disk Administrator to Configure Fault Tolerance

In this exercise, you will use a simulation program to implement disk striping with parity and disk mirroring. However, depending on your classroom setup, your instructor may direct you to use Disk Administrator instead.

Note Complete this exercise on your computer running Windows NT Server.

➤ **To configure disk striping with parity**

1. Click the Start button, point to Programs, point to Microsoft Windows NT 4.0 Core Technologies Training, point to Simulations, and then click Implementing Fault Tolerance Simulation.

Note If your computer running Windows NT Server has a minimum of three hard disks and available space for configuring the partitions, you may use Disk Administrator instead of the simulation program. To use Disk Administrator, start it from Administrative Tools.

2. Click an area of free space on Disk 0 to be used for creating a stripe set with parity.

3. Hold down the CTRL key and click an area of free space on Disk 1 and an area of free space on Disk 2.

4. On the **Fault Tolerance** menu, click **Create Stripe Set with Parity**.

   The **Create Stripe Set with Parity** dialog box appears. The default size is three times the size of the smallest area of selected free space.

5. In the **Create stripe set of total size** box, type **300** and then click **OK**.

   The partitions now have the same drive letter (G) and are highlighted in green. This indicates that they are part of a stripe set with parity.

ntoskrnl.exe file missing/corrupted

➤ **To configure disk mirroring**

1. To begin creating a mirror set, click drive D.

2. Hold down the CTRL key and click an area of free space on Disk 1.

    The area must be equal to or greater than the drive selected in the preceding step.

3. On the **Fault Tolerance** menu, click **Establish Mirror**.

    The partitions should now have the same drive letter (D) and be highlighted in purple. This indicates that they are part of a mirror set.

➤ **To exit and save changes**

1. On the **Partition** menu, click **Exit** to end the simulation.

    If you are running the simulation, you have completed the lab. If you are running Disk Administrator, continue with Steps 2 and 3.

2. When prompted to save your changes, click **Yes**.

3. When prompted to restart your computer, click **OK**.

Lab 12: Running Applications

Objectives

After completing this lab, you will be able to:

- Use Task Manager to view and manage active processes and applications.
- Determine the effects of a halted Windows-based 16-bit application.
- Run a Windows-based 16-bit application in its own memory space.
- Identify symptoms of missing subsystem files.
- Change the base priority of a process with Task Manager.

Estimated time to complete this lab: 50 minutes

Exercise 1
Using Task Manager

In this exercise, you will use Task Manager to view applications on your desktop and processes that execute in the background. You will also use Task Manager to terminate a process that has stopped responding.

Note Complete this exercise on your computer running Windows NT Server.

➤ **To run applications**

1. Open the D:\LabFiles\Apps folder.

2. In the Apps folder, start **Badapp32**, **Spind16**, and **Spind32**. Do not close the Apps folder.

3. Arrange your desktop so that you can see the Apps folder, Spind16, Spind32, and Badapp32 at the same time.

4. Click the SpinDIB:32 window, and then click **Open**.

5. Click **Billg**, and then click **Open**.

6. Click the SpinDIB:16 window, and then click **Open**.

7. Click **Billg**, and then click **OK**.

8. To verify that the SpinDIB:32 and SpinDIB:16 applications are running, on each application, click **Spin**!

➤ **To view running applications and system processes**

1. Press ctrl+alt+delete.

   A **Windows NT Security** dialog box appears.

2. Click **Task Manager**.

3. Click the **Applications** tab.

   What tasks are currently running?

   _____

   _____

4. Click the **Processes** tab.

   What processes are currently running?

   _____

   _____

   _____

Why does Spind16.exe appear indented under Ntvdm.exe?

_____

_____

What distinction is made in Task Manager between applications and processes?

_____

_____

_____

_____

5. In Task Manager, on the **Options** menu, click to clear Always on Top, so that it is not selected (that is, no check mark appears next to it).

➤ **To view the effects of a Win32-based application that has stopped responding**

1. On the Badapp32 Action menu, click **Hang**.

   In the Badapp32 window, the fuse burns down, and then the bomb explodes. At this point the application halts.

2. Move the mouse pointer over Badapp32.

   What is the status of Badapp32?

   _Hang_____

   _____

3. Switch to SpinDIB:32, and then to SpinDIB:16.

   Are SpinDIB:32 and SpinDIB:16 still active? (Can you spin Bill?)

   _YES_____

   _____

➤ **To terminate an application that has stopped responding**

1. Switch to Task Manager.

2. On the **Applications** tab, right-click **Badapp**.

3. Click **End Task**.

   A **Bad App** dialog box appears, indicating that the application cannot respond to the End Task request.

4. Click **End Task** to clear the dialog box and to end Badapp32.

   SpinDib:32 and SpinDIB:16 should still be running.

Exercise 2
Running Windows-based 16-bit Applications in the Same Address Space

In this exercise, you will observe the effects of a 16-bit application general protection fault (GP fault) error and the effects of a halted 16-bit application.

Note   Complete this exercise on your computer running Windows NT Server.

➤   **To observe the effects of a 16-bit application GP fault**

1. In the Apps folder, open Badapp16.

2. In the Badapp16 window, click the bomb.

   When the fuse burns down, the bomb explodes. At this point an error message occurs.

3. Do not click **Close** or **Ignore**.

4. Switch to SpinDIB:32.

   Is the application active? Why or why not?

   _____

   _____

5. Switch to SpinDIB:16.

   Is the application active? Why or why not?

   _____*No*_____

   _____

6. In the **Badapp16** dialog box containing the error message, click **Close**.

   An **Application Error** dialog box appears.

7. Click **Close**.

8. Switch to SpinDIB:16.

   Is the application active? Why or why not?

   _____*YES*_____

   _____

➤   **To observe the effects of a halted Windows-based 16-bit application**

1. With SpinDIB:32 and SpinDIB:16 still active, open Badapp16.

2. On the **Action** menu, click **Hang**.

    When the fuse burns down, the bomb explodes. At this point the application halts.

3. Move the mouse pointer over SpinDIB:16.

    What is the status of SpinDIB:16?

    _____ *Hang* _____

    _____

4. Move the mouse pointer over SpinDIB:32.

    What is the status of SpinDIB:32?

    _____ *active* _____

    _____

5. Use Task Manager to end the Badapp application.

6. Switch to SpinDIB:16 to verify that it is still active.

Exercise 3
Running a Windows-based 16-bit Application in a Separate Memory Space

In this exercise, you will run a Windows-based 16-bit application in its own memory space.

Note   Complete this exercise on your computer running Windows NT Server.

➤   **To create a shortcut that runs an application in a separate memory space**

1. Close SpinDIB:16.

2. In the Apps folder, right-click **Spind16**, and then click **Create Shortcut**.

    A new shortcut to Spind16 appears in the Apps folder.

3. Rename **Shortcut to Spind16** to **SpinDIB16 (separate WOW)**.

4. Right-click **SpinDIB16 (separate WOW)**, and then click **Properties**.

5. Click the **Shortcut** tab.

6. Click to select the **Run in Separate Memory Space** check box, and then click **OK**.

➤   **To observe the effects of an application running in a separate memory space**

1. Start SpinDIB16 (separate WOW).

    Notice that it takes somewhat longer to start SpinDIB:16 this time. This is because a new NTVDM and WOW must be loaded.

2. With SpinDIB:32 and SpinDIB:16 windows still active, start Badapp16.

3. Arrange your desktop so that you can see SpinDIB:16, SpinDIB:32, and Badapp at the same time.

4. On the Badapp **Action** menu, click **Hang**.

5. When Badapp stops responding, switch to SpinDIB:16.

    Is SpinDIB:16 still active? Why?

    _____

    _____

6. Use Task Manager to end the Badapp application.

7. Close SpinDIB:16, SpinDIB:32, Task Manager, LabFiles, and Apps.

Exercise 4
Observing the Effects of Missing Subsystem Files

In this exercise, you will rename key subsystem files, one at a time, and then observe the resulting effects on running MS-DOS-based, Win16-based, and Win32-based applications.

Note Complete this exercise on your computer running Windows NT Server.

➤ **To observe the effects of missing subsystem files**

1. Repeat steps 2–8 for each of the following subsystem files (one at a time):
   - D:\Winnt\System32\Ntvdm.exe
   - D:\Winnt\System32\Wowexec.exe
   - D:\Winnt\System32\Krnl386.exe

2. Rename the file, assigning an extension of .old

3. Shut down and restart Windows NT Server.

4. Log on as Administrator, and then start a Command Prompt.

5. In the D:\LabFiles\Apps directory, try to run Edit.com, and record the resulting behavior in the appropriate table that follows.

6. In D:\LabFiles\Apps directory, try to run Spind16.exe, and record the resulting behavior in the appropriate table that follows.

7. In the D:\LabFiles\Apps directory, try to run Spind32.exe, and record the resulting behavior in the appropriate table that follows.

8. Rename the subsystem file to its original name.

9. Shut down Windows NT Server, restart Windows NT Server, and then log on as Administrator.

Subsystem file: Ntvdm.exe	**Record results here**
Behavior when running Edit.com	
Behavior when running Spind16.exe	
Behavior when running Spind32.exe	

Subsystem file: Wowexec.exe	**Record results here**
Behavior when running Edit.com	
Behavior when running Spind16.exe	
Behavior when running Spind32.exe	

Subsystem file: Krnl386.exe	**Record results here**
Behavior when running Edit.com	
Behavior when running Spind16.exe	
Behavior when running Spind32.exe	

In which situations did Edit.com fail? Why?

_____

_____

In which situations did Spind16.exe fail? Why?

_____

_____

In which situations did Spind32.exe fail? Why?

_____

_____

Exercise 5
Changing Application Priorities

In this exercise, you will use Task Manager to alter the base priority of an active process.

Note   Complete this exercise on your computer running Windows NT Server.

➤   **To view the priority of a running application**

1. In the D:\LabFiles\Apps folder, start Counter.

2. Start a second instance of Counter.

3. Right-click the taskbar, and then click **Task Manager**.

4. Arrange Task Manager and the two Counters so that you can view them all on the screen.

5. In Task Manager, click the **Processes** tab.

6. On the **View** menu, click **Select Columns**.

7. Click to select the **Base Priority** check box, and then click **OK**.

8. If necessary, resize the Task Manager window until you can see the **Base Priority** column.

   At what priority is each Counter currently running?

> ➤   **To change the priority of a running application**

1. In Task Manager, on the **Processes** tab, right-click either instance of **Counter.exe**.

2. Point to **Set Priority**, and then click **Low**.

   A **Task Manager Warning** dialog box appears.

3. Click **Yes** to change the priority of this instance of Counter.exe.

   The low-priority instance of Counter.exe runs significantly slower than the normal-priority instance.

4. In Task Manager, on the **Processes** tab, right-click the instance of **Counter.exe** that is running with low priority.

5. Point to **Set Priority**, and then click **High**.

   A **Task Manager Warning** dialog box appears.

6. Click **Yes** to change the priority of this instance of Counter.exe.

   The high-priority instance of Counter.exe runs significantly faster than the normal-priority instance.

7. Use Task Manager to end both instances of Counter.

8. Close Task Manager and the Apps and LabFiles folders.

Lab 13: Installing NWLink

Objective

After completing this lab, you will be able to:

Install the Microsoft NWLink Internetwork Packet Exchange/Sequenced Packet Exchange (IPX/SPX) Compatible Transport protocol.

Test the Microsoft NWLink IPX/SPX Compatible Transport protocol installation.

Estimated time to complete this lab: 10 minutes

Exercise 1
Installing NWLink

In this exercise, you will install NWLink. You will then test your ability to connect to the Instructor computer.

Note   Complete this exercise on your computer running Windows NT Server.

➤ **To install NWLink**

1.   Start the Network program.

   The **Network** dialog box opens.

2.   Click the **Protocols** tab, and then click **Add**.

   The **Select Network Protocol** dialog box appears.

3.   Click **NWLink IPX/SPX Compatible Transport**, and then click **OK**.

   The **Windows NT Setup** dialog box appears, prompting you for the path of the files to be copied.

4.   Type **\\Instructor\Ntsrv** and then click **Continue**.

   All the files that you need are copied to your computer.

   What are the two new protocols displayed on the **Protocols** tab of the **Network** dialog box?

   NWLink IPX / SPX Compatible transport
   NWLink NetBios

5.   Click **TCP/IP Protocol**, and then click **Remove**.

   A **Warning** dialog box appears, indicating that this action will permanently remove the component from the system. If you wish to reinstall it, you will have to restart the system before doing so.

6.   Click **Yes**, and then click **Close**.

   The installation and binding process continues, and the **Network Settings Change** dialog box appears, asking if you want to restart your computer.

7.   Click **Yes** to restart Windows NT Server.

➤ **To test your installation of NWLink**

1.   Log on as Administrator.

   Can you connect to \\Instructor\Ntsrv?

2.   Disconnect from \\Instructor\Ntsrv.

Lab 14: Installing NetBEUI

Objective

After completing this lab, you will be able to:

Install NetBIOS extended user interface (NetBEUI).

Verify that the installation was successful.

Before You Begin

Prerequisite

Lab 13: Installing NWLink.

Estimated time to complete this lab: 10 minutes

Exercise 1
Installing NetBEUI

In this exercise, you will install NetBEUI and remove NWLink. You will then test your ability to connect to the Instructor computer.

Note Complete this exercise on your computer running Windows NT Server.

➤ **To install NetBEUI**

1. Start the Network program.

   The **Network** dialog box appears.

2. Click the **Protocols** tab, and then click **Add**.

3. Click **NetBEUI Protocol**, and then click **OK**.

   A **Windows NT Setup** dialog box appears, prompting you for the path of the files to be copied.

4. Type **\\Instructor\Ntsrv** and then click **Continue**.

   Once the NetBEUI protocol is installed, the **Protocols** tab of the **Network** dialog box shows that the following three protocols are currently installed:

   NetBEUI Protocol

   NWLink IPX/SPX Compatible Transport

   NWLink NetBIOS

5. Click **NWLink IPX/SPX Compatible Transport**, and then click **Remove**.

   A **Warning** dialog box appears, indicating that this action will permanently remove the component from the system and asking if you still want to continue.

6. Click **Yes**, and then click **Close**.

   The installation and binding process continues, and the **Network Settings Change** dialog box appears, asking if you want to restart your computer.

7. Click **Yes** to restart Windows NT Server.

➤ **To verify that your installation was successful**

1. Log on as Administrator.

   Can you connect to \\Instructor\Ntsrv?

   _____YES_____

2. Disconnect from \\Instructor\Ntsrv.

Lab 15: Configuring TCP/IP

Objectives

After completing this lab, you will be able to:

- Manually configure Transmission Control Protocol/Internet Protocol (TCP/IP) parameters on a computer running Windows NT.
- Use **ping** to verify IP connectivity.
- Automatically configure TCP/IP by using Dynamic Host Configuration Protocol (DHCP).
- Use File Transfer Protocol (FTP) to transfer a file from the FTP server.

Before You Begin

Before beginning this lab, your instructor should assign each student an IP address to be used in this lab. Record your assigned IP address below.

_____._____._____._____

Use your assigned IP address to replace the *w.x.y.z* placeholder in the lab.

This lab assumes that the Instructor computer has an IP address of 131.107.2.200. If it is different, your instructor will tell you, and you should substitute the correct address for the Instructor computer, where appropriate, throughout this lab.

Estimated time to complete this lab: 20 minutes

Exercise 1
Manually Configuring TCP/IP on a Computer Running Windows NT 4.0

In this exercise, you will manually configure the TCP/IP parameters on a computer running Windows NT.

Note   Complete this exercise on your computer running Windows NT Server.

➤ **To create a shortcut**

1. Log on as Administrator, and then in Control Panel, drag the Network icon to your desktop.

   A **Shortcut** dialog box appears, asking if you want to create a Shortcut.

2. Click **Yes**.

➤ **To manually configure TCP/IP**

1. tSart the Network program.

   The **Network** dialog box appears.

2. Click the **Protocols** tab.

3. Click **TCP/IP Protocol**, and then click **Properties**.

4. Click the **IP Address** tab, click **Specify an IP address**, and then enter the following information.

In this box	Use	
IP Address	131.107.2.200	(Unless instructed otherwise)
Subnet Mask	255.255.255.0	(Unless instructed otherwise)
Default Gateway	Leave blank	(Unless instructed otherwise)

5. Click **OK**.

   A **System Process—System Error** dialog box appears, displaying the following message:

   ```
   The system has detected an IP address conflict with another system on
   the network. The local interface has been disabled. More details are
   available in the system event log. Consult your network administrator
   to resolve the conflict.
   ```

   Why does this message appear?

   causing IP conflict

6. Click **OK**.

➤ **To specify a correct address**

1. In the **Network** dialog box, click the **Protocols** tab.

2. Click **TCP/IP Protocol**, and then click **Properties**.

3. Click the **IP Address** tab, click **Specify an IP address**, and then enter the following information.

In this box	Use	
IP Address	*w.x.y.z*	(Unless instructed otherwise)
Subnet Mask	**255.255.255.0**	(Unless instructed otherwise)
Default Gateway	Leave blank	(Unless instructed otherwise)

4. Click **OK** to close the **Properties** dialog box.

5. Click **OK** to close the **Network** dialog box.

6. Shut down and restart Windows NT Server.

Exercise 2
Using Ping to Verify IP Connectivity

In this exercise, you will use **ping** to verify that the TCP/IP configuration is correct.

Note   Complete this exercise on your computer running Windows NT Server.

➤ **To verify that the TCP/IP configuration is correct**

1. Log on as Administrator.

2. Start a Command Prompt.

3. To test that IP is working and bound to your adapter, type **ping 127.0.0.1** and then press ENTER.

   This internal loop-back test should give you four replies if TCP/IP is bound to the adapter.

4. To test TCP/IP connectivity with the Instructor computer, type **ping 131.107.2.200** and then press ENTER.

   Four "Reply from 131.107.2.200" messages should appear.

5. Try pinging other computers in your classroom.

Exercise 3
Automatically Configuring TCP/IP on a Computer Running Windows NT 4.0

In this exercise, you will configure your computer running Windows NT Server to obtain its IP addressing information from a DHCP server, and then view the addressing information supplied to your computer by the DHCP server.

Note   Complete this exercise on your computer running Windows NT Server.

➤ **To automatically configure TCP/IP by using DHCP**

In this procedure, you will configure your computer running Windows NT Server to use DHCP to obtain a TCP/IP address.

1. Start the Network program.

2. Click the **Protocols** tab, click **TCP/IP Protocol**, and then click **Properties**.

3. Click the **IP Address** tab, and then click **Obtain an IP address from a DHCP server**.

   A **Microsoft TCP/IP** dialog box appears, indicating that the DHCP protocol will attempt to automatically configure the computer during system initialization.

4. Click **Yes**.

5. Click **OK** to close the **Microsoft TCP/IP Properties** dialog box, and then click **OK** to close the **Network** dialog box.

➤ **To verify the DHCP configuration**

In this procedure, you will verify the Windows NT Server configuration of TCP/IP from the DHCP server.

1. Switch to a Command Prompt.

2. To test TCP/IP connectivity with the Instructor computer, type **ping 131.107.2.200** and then press ENTER.

   Four "Reply from 131.107.2.200" messages should appear.

   Note   If you did not receive four successful replies, contact your instructor.

3. To verify the DHCP-assigned TCP/IP parameters for your computer, type **ipconfig /all** and then press ENTER.

The TCP/IP configuration information appears. It should look similar to the information shown in the following two tables.

Windows NT IP configuration

Host name	server1
DNS servers	131.107.2.200
Node type	Hybrid
NetBIOS scope ID	
IP routing enabled	No
WINS proxy enable	No
NetBIOS resolution	No

Ethernet adapter IEEPRO1

Description	Intel EtherExpress PRO
Physical address	00-AA-00-61-3D-BE
DHCP enabled	Yes
IP address	131.107.2.150
Subnet mask	255.255.255.0
Default gateway	
DHCP server	131.107.2.200
Primary WINS server	131.107.2.200
Secondary WINS server	
Lease obtained	Wednesday, July 17, 1996 12:35:00 PM
Lease expires	Tuesday, August 05, 1996 1:31:48 PM

What is the IP address that the DHCP server assigned to your computer?

_____

What is the IP address of the DHCP server?

_____

Exercise 4
Transferring a File with FTP

In this exercise, you will transfer a file from the FTP server to your computer using the FTP client software on your domain controller running Windows NT Server.

Note Complete this exercise on your computer running Windows NT Server.

➤ **To transfer a file using FTP**

1. Switch to a Command Prompt.

2. Type **ftp** and then press ENTER.

   An ftp> prompt appears.

3. At the ftp> prompt, type **open** and then press ENTER.

   A (to) prompt appears.

4. At the (to) prompt, type **instructor** and then press ENTER.

   A User (instructor:(none)) prompt appears.

5. At the User (instructor:(none)) prompt, type **anonymous** and then press ENTER.

   A Password: prompt appears.

6. At the Password: prompt, press ENTER for no password.

   A User logged in message appears, followed by an ftp> prompt.

7. At the ftp> prompt, type **get getme.txt** and then press ENTER.

   The Getme.txt file is copied to the local drive.

8. At the ftp> prompt, type **close** and then press ENTER.

   The FTP session to the FTP server is canceled.

9. To exit FTP, at the ftp> prompt, type **bye** and then press ENTER.

10. Verify that the Getme.txt file exists on your local disk.

    Where did FTP put Getme.txt?

---

11. Close the Command Prompt.

Lab 16: Installing and Configuring DHCP

Objectives

After completing this lab, you will be able to:

- Install and configure a Dynamic Host Configuration Protocol (DHCP) server.
- Test the DHCP server configuration.
- Troubleshoot various DHCP server configuration errors.

Before You Begin

In this lab, you will work with a partner. Initially, both computers will be running Windows NT Server to enable both you and your partner to practice installing and configuring a DHCP server. In Exercises 3 and 4, one computer will be started as a computer running Windows NT Workstation to test the DHCP server. At the end of the lab, you will be able to reverse roles to test the other DHCP server.

Before beginning this lab, record your assigned IP address below. (If you do not remember your assigned IP address, look it up in Lab 15: Configuring TCP/IP.)

_____._____._____._____

Use your IP address to replace the *w.x.y.z* placeholder in the lab.

Record your partner's assigned IP address below.

_____._____._____._____

Use your partner's assigned IP address to replace the *your partner's IP address* placeholder in the lab.

You will also need to know your partner's assigned student number.

Estimated time to complete this lab: 45 minutes

Exercise 1
Installing TCP/IP

In this exercise, you will reinstall TCP/IP and remove any other network protocol currently installed.

Note Complete this exercise on your computer running Windows NT Server.

➤ **To reinstall TCP/IP and remove all other network protocols**

1. Log on as Administrator.

2. Start the Network program.

   The **Network** dialog box appears.

3. Install TCP/IP Protocol.

   - When prompted, do not elect to use DHCP.

   - Enter the configuration settings shown in the following table.

In this box	Use
IP Address	*w.x.y.z* (assigned by your instructor)
Subnet Mask	**255.255.255.0** (unless instructed otherwise)
Default Gateway	Leave blank (unless instructed otherwise)

4. When prompted to restart your computer, click **No**.

5. Remove all other network protocols, such as NetBEUI.

6. When prompted to restart your computer, click **Yes** to restart Windows NT Server.

Exercise 2
Installing and Configuring a DHCP Server

In this exercise, you will install and configure a DHCP server to automatically assign TCP/IP configuration information to DHCP clients.

Note Complete this exercise on your computer running Windows NT Server.

➤ **To install the DHCP Server service**

1. Log on as Administrator.

2. Start the Network program.

   The **Network** dialog box appears.

3. Click the **Services** tab.

4. Click **Add**.

   The **Select Network Services** dialog box appears.

5. Click **Microsoft DHCP Server**, and then click **OK**.

6. When prompted for the path of the Windows NT distribution files, type **\\instructor\ntsrv** and then click **Continue**.

   The appropriate files are copied to your computer and a dialog box appears, stating that if any adapters are using DHCP to obtain an IP address, they are now required to use a static IP address.

7. Click **OK**, and then click **Close**.

8. Click **Yes** to restart Windows NT Server.

➤ **To determine DHCP service names**

In this procedure, you use the Services program in Control Panel to determine the names of the two DHCP services.

1. Log on as Administrator.

2. In Control Panel, double-click the Services icon.

   What are the names of the two DHCP-related services?

   DHCP Clent, MS DHCP Server

   What are the **Status** and **Startup** values for these two services?

   disabled   Automatic

3. Close Services.

➤   **To create a DHCP scope**

In this procedure, you will create a DHCP scope that consists of one IP address (your partner's) with an assigned lease time of one day.

1. Click the **Start** button, point to **Programs**, point to **Administrative Tools (Common)**, and then click **DHCP Manager**.

   The DHCP Manager window appears.

2. Click **Scope**.

   Notice that no options on the menu are available.

3. Under **DHCP Servers**, double-click *Local Machine*.

   Notice that **(Local)** now appears on the title bar for DHCP Manager.

4. On the **Scope** menu, click **Create**.

   The **Create Scope** dialog box appears.

5. Configure the scope using the information in the following table.

In this box	Type this
IP Address Pool Start Address	*your partner's IP address*
IP Address Pool End Address	*your partner's IP address*
Subnet Mask	**255.255.255.0** (unless instructed otherwise)
Lease Duration Limited To (Days)	**1**

6. When you are finished, click **OK**.

   A **DHCP Manager** dialog box appears, indicating that the scope was successfully created, and now needs to be activated.

7. Click **No** so that the scope is not activated.

   A **DHCP Manager** dialog box appears, stating that no more data is available.

8. Click **OK**.

   The DHCP Manager window appears with the new scope added. Notice the gray light bulb next to the IP address, indicating an inactive scope.

➤ **To configure a DHCP scope option**

In this procedure, you will create a DHCP scope option that automatically assigns a default gateway address to DHCP clients.

1. On the **DHCP Options** menu, click **Scope**.

   The **DHCP Options: Scope** dialog box appears.

2. Under **Unused Options**, click **003 Router**, and then click **Add**.

   The **003 Router** option appears in the **Active Options** box.

3. Click **Value**.

   The **DHCP Options: Scope** dialog box expands to add the **IP Address** box.

4. Click **Edit Array**.

   The **IP Address Array Editor** dialog box appears.

5. In the **New IP Address** box, type your default gateway address (131.107.2.200 unless instructed otherwise), and then click **Add**.

   The new IP address appears under **IP Addresses**.

6. Click **OK**.

7. In the **DHCP Options: Scope** dialog box, click **OK**.

   A **DHCP Manager** dialog box appears, indicating that there is no more data.

8. Click **OK** to close the **DHCP Manager** dialog box.

➤ **To add a client lease reservation**

In this procedure, you will create a reservation for your partner's computer, and then activate the scope. This will ensure that each DHCP server is able to lease an address to a unique DHCP client in an environment of multiple DHCP servers (as in the classroom environment).

1. Open a Command Prompt window, and then ping *your partner's IP address*.

2. Type **arp -a** and then press ENTER to obtain the physical address of your partner's network adapter. Record the address here for reference.

   _00 - e0 - df - 39 - 08 - f4_

3. Switch to DHCP Manager.

4. On the **Scope** menu, click **Add Reservations**.

   The **Add Reserved Clients** dialog box appears.

5. In the **IP Address** box, type *your partner's IP address*.

6. In the **Unique Identifier** box, type the physical address (without the hyphens) of your partner's network adapter.

7. In the **Client Name** box, type **Workstation**x (where *x* is your partner's assigned student number), and then click **Add**.

8. Click **Close** to return to DHCP Manager.

9. On the **Scope** menu, click **Activate** to activate the scope.

   Notice the light bulb is now yellow, indicating an active scope.

Exercise 3
Testing the DHCP Configuration

In Exercises 3 and 4, you will be working with your partner to test the DHCP server configuration. One computer will be running Windows NT Server and the DHCP Server service, and the other computer will be restarted as Windows NT Workstation.

Note Complete this exercise only on the computer running Windows NT Workstation.

➤ **To test the DHCP server configuration**

1. Shut down one computer running Windows NT Server, and then restart it as Windows NT Workstation.

2. Log on to the domain as Administrator.

3. Start a Command Prompt.

4. Type **ipconfig /release** and then press ENTER to release the existing IP address.

5. Type **ipconfig /renew** and then press ENTER to request a new IP address from a DHCP server on the network.

6. Type **ipconfig /all** and then press ENTER to view the new TCP/IP configuration.

   What IP address was assigned to the computer running Windows NT Workstation by the DHCP server?

   _121 - 107 . 2 . 156_

   What is the DHCP server address?

   _181 . 107 . 2 . 200 ._

   What is the address of the default gateway?

   _0 . 0 . 0 . 0_

Exercise 4
Troubleshooting DHCP

In this exercise, you will troubleshoot various DHCP configuration errors.

Note This exercise contains procedures for both computers. Make sure that you complete the correct procedure on the correct computer.

➤ **To view DHCP assigned addresses**

In this procedure, you will view the list of leased addresses on a DHCP server.

Note Complete this procedure only on the computer running Windows NT Server.

1. In DHCP Manager, double-click ***Local Machine***.

2. Click the local scope.

3. On the **Scope** menu, click **Active Leases**.

    The **Active Leases** dialog box appears, displaying the list of IP addresses that have been leased to clients.

4. Click **Properties**.

    The **Client Properties** dialog box appears. Note that the **Lease Expires** time is infinite for a client reservation.

5. Click **Cancel** to return to the **Active Leases** dialog box.

6. Click **Cancel** to return to DHCP Manager.

7. Close DHCP Manager.

➤ **To renew a DHCP lease**

In this procedure, you will renew the lease assigned to the computer running Windows NT Workstation.

Note Complete this procedure only on the computer running Windows NT Workstation.

1. Switch to the Command Prompt.

2. Type **ipconfig /all** and then press ENTER to view the lease information.

   When does the lease expire?

   Friday, August 13, 1999 9:07:23 PM

3. Type **ipconfig /release** and then press ENTER.

4. Type **ipconfig /all** and then press ENTER to view the lease information.

   What is your IP address?

   0.0.0.0

5. Type **ipconfig /renew** and then press ENTER to renew the lease.

   The Windows NT IP configuration information for the assigned address is displayed.

6. Type **ipconfig /all** and then press ENTER to view the lease information again.

   When does the lease expire?

   Fr, Aug 13, 1999 9:02:27 PM

➤ **To stop the DHCP Server service**

In this procedure, you will stop the DHCP Server service to prevent IP address lease assignments and renewals.

Note Complete this procedure only on the computer running Windows NT Server.

1. In Control Panel, double-click the Services icon.

2. Click **Microsoft DHCP Server**, and then click **Stop**.

3. Click **Yes** when prompted.

   The DHCP Server service stops.

➤   **To attempt lease renewal when the DHCP server is unavailable**

In this procedure, you will use **ipconfig** to attempt to renew the lease assigned to the computer running Windows NT Workstation while the DHCP server is unavailable.

Note   Complete this procedure only on the computer running Windows NT Workstation.

1. At a Command Prompt, type **ipconfig /renew** and then press ENTER.

    Could you successfully renew the lease?

    No   YES ?

2. Use **ping** to verify that TCP/IP can communicate with the Instructor computer, for which the IP address is 131.107.2.200.

    Ping should respond with four success messages.

    Even though you were unable to renew your IP address lease, it is still a valid lease (it has not expired), so TCP/IP communications are still possible.

➤   **To release a DHCP address**

In this procedure, you will use **ipconfig** to release the IP address lease assigned to the computer running Windows NT Workstation.

Note   Complete this procedure only on the computer running Windows NT Workstation.

1. At a Command Prompt, type **ipconfig /release** and then press ENTER.

    The Windows NT IP configuration information appears.

    What message did you receive?

    IP address 191.107.2.156 successfully released for adapter "RTL 8029"

2. Use **ping** to test TCP/IP communications with the Instructor computer.

    Ping should respond with four *Destination host unreachable* messages.

3. Shut down and restart Windows NT Workstation.

4. Log on to the domain as Administrator.

    A **Logon Message** dialog box appears, stating that a domain controller could not be found.

    Why does this message appear?

5. Click **OK** to close the **Logon Message** dialog box.

6. At a Command Prompt, use **ipconfig /all** to view the IP configuration.

   What is the IP address? Why?

   0. 0. 0. 0

➤ **To start the DHCP Server service**

In this procedure, you will start the DHCP Server service to allow IP address lease assignments and renewals.

Note Complete this procedure only on the computer running Windows NT Server.

■ Use either the Services program in Control Panel, or use Server Manager to start the DHCP Server service.

➤ **To renew a DHCP lease**

In this procedure, you will use **ipconfig** to renew the lease assigned to the computer running Windows NT Workstation.

Note Complete this procedure only on the computer running Windows NT Workstation.

1. At a Command Prompt, type **ipconfig /renew** and then press ENTER.

   The Windows NT IP configuration information for the assigned address is displayed.

2. Type **ipconfig /all** and then press ENTER.

   When does the lease expire?

   Fri, Aug 13, 99 9:21:07 PM

3. Shut down and restart your computer as Windows NT Server.

Lab 17: Installing and Configuring WINS

Objectives

After completing this lab, you will be able to:

- Install a Windows Internet Name Service (WINS) server.
- Configure a DHCP server for WINS.

Before You Begin

In this lab, you will work with a partner. Initially, both computers will be running Windows NT Server to enable both you and your partner to practice installing and configuring a WINS server. In Exercise 3, one computer will be started as a computer running Windows NT Workstation to test the WINS server. At the end of the lab, you will be able to reverse roles to test the other WINS server.

Before beginning this lab, record your assigned IP address below.

_131_ . _107_. _2_ . _3_

Use your IP address to replace the *your IP address* placeholder in the lab.

Prerequisite

Lab 16: Installing and Configuring DHCP.

Estimated time to complete this lab: 30 minutes

Exercise 1
Installing a WINS Server

In this exercise, you will install a WINS server to automatically resolve NetBIOS names to IP addresses for WINS clients.

Note   Complete this exercise on your computer running Windows NT Server.

➤ **To install the WINS Server service**

1. Log on as Administrator.

2. Start the Network program, and then click the **Services** tab.

3. Click **Add**.

   The **Select Network Service** dialog box appears.

4. Click **Windows Internet Name Service**, and then click **OK**.

   A **Windows NT Setup** dialog box appears, asking for the full path to the software.

5. Type **\\Instructor\Ntsrv** and then click **Continue**.

6. Click the **Protocols** tab.

7. Double-click **TCP/IP Protocol**.

   The **Microsoft TCP/IP Properties** dialog box appears.

8. Click the **WINS Address** tab.

9. In the **Primary WINS Server** box, type *your IP address* and then click **OK**.

   The **Network** dialog box appears.

10. Click **Close**.

    A **Network Settings Change** dialog box appears, indicating that the computer needs to be restarted to initialize the new configuration.

11. Click **Yes** to restart Windows NT Server.

Exercise 2
Configuring a DHCP Server for WINS

In this exercise, you will configure the DHCP server to automatically assign the WINS server address and NetBIOS node types to DHCP clients.

Note Complete this exercise on your computer running Windows NT Server.

➤ **To configure the DHCP server to assign WINS server addresses**

1. Log on as Administrator.

2. On the **Administrative Tools (Common)** menu, click **DHCP Manager**.

   DHCP Manager appears.

3. Double-click *****Local Machine*****.

   The IP address for the local scope appears.

4. Click the IP address for the local scope.

   The local scope options appear under **Option Configuration**.

5. On the **DHCP Options** menu, click **Scope**.

   The **DHCP Options: Scope** dialog box appears.

6. Under **Unused Options**, click **044 WINS/NBNS Servers**, and then click **Add**.

   A **DHCP Manager** dialog box appears, indicating that for WINS to function properly, you must add the option **046 WINS/NBT Node Type**.

7. Click **OK**.

   The **044 WINS/NBNS Servers** option now appears selected under **Active Options**.

8. Click **Value**.

   The **DHCP Scope: Options** dialog box expands.

9. Click **Edit Array**.

   The **IP Address Array Editor** dialog box appears.

10. Under **New IP Address**, type *your IP address* and then click **Add**.

   The new IP address appears under **IP Addresses**.

11. Click **OK** to return to the **DHCP Options: Scope** dialog box.

12. Under **Unused Options**, click **046 WINS/NBT Node Type**, and then click **Add**.

   The **046 WINS/NBT Node Type** option now appears under **Active Options**.

13. In the **Byte** box, type **0x8** and then click **OK**.

   DHCP Manager appears. Under **Option Configuration**, the following active scope options appear: **003 Router**, **044 WINS/NBNS Servers**, and **046 WINS/NBT Node Type**.

14. Exit DHCP Manager.

Exercise 3
Testing the WINS and DHCP Server Configuration

In this exercise, you will work with a partner to test the WINS and DHCP server configuration. One computer will be running Windows NT Server and the other computer will be restarted as Windows NT Workstation.

Note Complete this exercise on the computer running Windows NT Workstation.

➤ **To test the configuration of the DHCP server to assign WINS server addresses**

1. Shut down one computer running Windows NT Server, and restart the computer as Windows NT Workstation.

2. Log on to the domain as Administrator.

3. Start a Command Prompt.

4. Type **ipconfig /renew** and then press ENTER to request a new IP address from a DHCP server on the network.

5. Type **ipconfig /all** and then press ENTER to view the new TCP/IP configuration.

   What is the IP address of the primary WINS server?

   _181. 107. 2. 200_

   What is the node type?

   Hybrid

6. Type **ping instructor** and then press ENTER.

   Why were you successful in pinging a NetBIOS computer name?

   _____

   _____

7. Shut down and restart your computer as Windows NT Server.

Exercise 4
Reversing Roles *(if time permits)*

In this exercise, you and your partner will reverse roles to test the configuration.

➤ **To reverse roles**

1. Restart the computer running Windows NT Server as Windows NT Workstation.

Repeat Exercise 3.

Lab 18: Installing and Configuring DNS

Objectives

After completing this lab, you will be able to:

- Install the Domain Name System (DNS) Server service.
- Configure a DNS server.
- Resolve host names to IP addresses by using DNS.

Before You Begin

In this lab, you will work with a partner, configuring your DNS server to resolve references to your partner's computer. Both you and your partner will complete all exercises.

Your computer must be configured with a static IP address. If your computer running Windows NT Server is currently leasing an address from a DHCP server, obtain a static IP address from your instructor.

Record your assigned IP address below.

_____._____._____._____

Use your IP address to replace the *your IP address* placeholder in the lab.

Record your partner's assigned IP address below.

_____._____._____._____

Use your partner's assigned IP address to replace the *your partner's IP address* placeholder in the lab.

You will also need the following information to complete this lab:

- Your assigned student number.
- Your partner's assigned student number.
- Your partner's Windows NT Server computer name.

Prerequisite

Lab 16: Installing and Configuring DHCP, or your computer running Windows NT Server must be configured with a static IP address.

Estimated time to complete this lab: 20 minutes

Exercise 1
Installing the DNS Server Service

In this exercise, you will install the DNS Server service and configure the DNS Server service search order.

Note   Complete this exercise on your computer running Windows NT Server.

➤   **To install the DNS Server service**

1. Log on as Administrator.
2. Start the Network program, and then click the **Services** tab.
3. Click **Add**.

    The **Select Network Service** dialog box appears.
4. In the **Network Service** list, click **Microsoft DNS Server**, and then click **OK**.

    Windows NT Setup displays a dialog box asking for the path to the Windows NT distribution files.
5. Type **\\Instructor\Ntsrv** and then click **Continue**.

    All necessary files, including the sample files, are copied to your hard disk.
6. In the **Network** dialog box, click the **Protocols** tab.
7. Double-click **TCP/IP Protocol**.
8. Click the **DNS** tab.
9. In the **Domain** box, type **corpx.com** (where *x* is your assigned student number), and then click **OK**.
10. In the **Network** dialog box, click **Close**.
11. When prompted, click **Yes** to restart Windows NT Server.

➤ **To configure the DNS Server service search order**

1. Log on as Administrator.

2. Start the Network program, and then click the **Protocols** tab.

3. Double-click **TCP/IP Protocol**.

4. Click the **DNS** tab.

5. In the **DNS Service Search Order** box, click **Add**.

6. In the **DNS Server** box, type *your IP address* and then click **Add**.

7. Click **OK**.

   The **Network** dialog box appears.

8. Click **OK** to close the **Network** dialog box.

Exercise 2
Configuring a DNS Server

In this exercise, you will configure a primary zone.

Note Complete this exercise on your computer running Windows NT Server.

➤ **To configure the DNS Server service**

1. Click the **Start** button, point to **Programs**, point to **Administrative Tools (Common)**, and then click **DNS Manager**.

2. On the **DNS** menu, click **New Server**.

   The **Add DNS Server** dialog box appears.

3. In the **DNS Server** box, type **Server**x (where x is your assigned student number), and then click **OK**.

4. Right-click your computer name, and then click **New Zone**.

   The **Creating New Zone for Server**x dialog box appears.

5. Click **Primary**, and then click **Next**.

6. In the **Zone Name** box, type **corp**x**.com** (where x is your assigned student number).

7. Press the TAB key.

   Corp$x$**.com.dns** is automatically entered in the **Zone File** box.

8. Click **Next**, and then click **Finish**.

   Notice that the **Server List** now has a zone name, **corp**x**.com**. In the right pane, notice the **Zone Info** entries that have been added.

Exercise 3
Using DNS to Resolve IP Addresses

In this exercise, you will add a host name, an alias for your partner's computer, and a Name Server record for your partner's computer to your domain. The alias will be used to test whether name resolution is being completed by WINS or DNS. The alias name will exist only in the DNS entries, and not in the WINS database.

Note Complete this exercise on your computer running Windows NT Server.

➤ **To add your partner's computer as a New Host in your domain**

1. In the left pane of DNS Manager, right-click your zone name, **corp***x***.com**.

2. On the menu that appears, click **New Host**.

   The **New Host** dialog box appears.

3. In the **Host Name** box, type your partner's computer name, **Server***x* (where *x* is your partner's assigned student number).

4. In the **Host IP Address** box, type *your partner's IP address* and then click **Add Host**.

5. Click **Done**.

➤ **To add an alias for your partner's computer to your zone**

1. In the left pane, right-click your zone name.

2. On the menu that appears, click **New Record**.

   The **New Resource Record** dialog box appears.

3. Under **Record Type**, click **CNAME Record**.

4. In the **Alias Name** box, type **srv***x* (where *x* is your partner's assigned student number).

5. In the **For Host DNS Name** box, type *your partner's computer name* followed by a **.** (period), followed by *your DNS domain name*.

   For example, if your partner's assigned student number is 6 and your assigned student number is 5, you would type the following:

   Server6.corp5.com

6. Click **OK**.

   Note A CNAME Record is also known as an alias name.

➤   **To add a Name Server record to your domain**

1. In the left pane, right-click your zone name.

2. On the menu that appears, click **New Record**.

    The **New Resource Record** dialog box appears.

3. Under **Record Type**, click **NS Record**.

    Notice that the domain is already filled in with your domain name.

4. In the **Name Server DNS Name** box, type *your partner's computer's name*, **Server***x* (where *x* is your partner's assigned student number).

5. Click **OK**.

6. Close DNS Manager.

➤   **To resolve an IP address using DNS**

1. Start a Command Prompt.

2. Type **ping srv***x* (where *x* is your partner's assigned student number), and then press ENTER.

    What IP address did it return ?

    <u>SERVER10. corp09. com</u>

Close the Command Prompt.

Lab 19: Installing Remote Access Service

Objectives

After completing this lab, you will be able to:

- Install and configure Remote Access Service (RAS).
- Create a phonebook entry.
- Test the RAS installation.
- Remove RAS.

Before You Begin

In this lab, you will work with a partner. One partner will start his or her computer running Windows NT Workstation.

You will need to know your partner's assigned student number.

You will need a null modem cable to complete this lab.

Your instructor will assign you an IP address range and a COM port to use in this lab.

Prerequisites

Lab 5: Using Control Panel, to create an on-the-network hardware profile.

Lab 6: Implementing System Policies, to create a logon message.

Estimated time to complete this lab: 30 minutes

Exercise 1
Installing and Configuring RAS

In this exercise, you will install RAS. One computer will be running Windows NT Server and the other computer will be running Windows NT Workstation.

➤ **To prepare your computer**

Note Complete this procedure on the computer running Windows NT Workstation.

- Shut down one of your computers running Windows NT Server, and then restart it as Windows NT Workstation.

➤ **To install RAS**

Note Complete this procedure on both computers. One computer should be running Windows NT Server and the other computer should be running Windows NT Workstation.

1. Log on as Administrator.
2. Start the Network program.
3. Click the **Services** tab, and then click **Add**.
4. In the **Select Network Service** dialog box, click **Remote Access Service**, and then click **OK**.
5. When prompted for the path to the distribution files, do one of the following:

   If you are working on the computer running Windows NT Server, type **\\Instructor\Ntsrv** and then click **Continue**.

   – or –

   If you are working on the computer running Windows NT Workstation, type **\\Instructor\Ntwks** and then click **Continue**.

   The RAS files will be copied to your computer.

   A **Remote Access Setup** dialog box appears, stating that there are no RAS capable devices to add, and asking if you want RAS Setup to invoke the modem installer to enable you to add a modem.

6. Click **Yes**.

   The Install New Modem wizard appears.

7. Click to select the **Don't detect my modem; I will select it from a list** check box, and then click **Next**.

   The Install New Modem wizard continues.

8. Under **Manufacturers**, click **(Standard Modem Types)**.

9. Under **Models**, click **Dial-Up Networking Serial Cable between 2 PCs**, and then click **Next**.

   The Install New Modem wizard continues.

10. Click **Selected Ports**, click **COM1** (your instructor may supply you with a different COM port), and then click **Next**.

11. In the **Location Information** dialog box, click the appropriate country under **What country are you in now**?.

12. In the **What area (or city) code are you in now?** box, type your area code.

13. Click **Next**.

14. Click **Finish**.

    The **Add RAS Device** dialog box appears. You should see the entry **COM1-Dial-up Networking Serial Cable between 2 PCs** in the **RAS Capable Devices** list.

15. Click **OK**.

➤   **To configure port usage**

Note Complete this procedure on both computers. One computer should be running Windows NT Server and the other computer should be running Windows NT Workstation.

---

1. In the **Remote Access Setup** dialog box, click **Configure**.

   The **Configure Port Usage** dialog box appears.

2. Click **Dial Out and Receive Calls**, and then click **OK**.

   The **Remote Access Setup** dialog box appears.

3. Click **Network**.

   The **Network Configuration** dialog box appears.

4. Under **Dial Out Protocols**, select the **NetBEUI**, **TCP/IP**, and **IPX** check boxes.

5. Under **Server Settings**, select the **NetBEUI, TCP/IP**, and **IPX** check boxes.

> **Note**   Computers running Windows NT Server include the option to enable multilink.

6. Next to **NetBEUI**, click **Configure**.

   The **RAS Server NetBEUI Configuration** dialog box appears.

7. Click **Entire Network**, and then click **OK**.

8. Next to **TCP/IP**, click **Configure**.

   The **RAS Server TCP/IP Configuration** dialog box appears.

9. Under **Allow remote TCP/IP clients to access**, click **Entire Network**.

10. Click **Use static address pool**.

11. Type in the beginning and ending values for the IP address range assigned by your instructor, and then click **OK**.

12. Next to **IPX**, click **Configure**.

    The **RAS Server IPX Configuration** dialog box appears.

13. Under **Allow remote IPX clients to access**, click **Entire network**.

14. Click **Allocate network numbers automatically**.

15. Click to select the **Assign same network number to all IPX clients** check box, and then click **OK**.

16. Click **OK** to close the **Network Configuration** dialog box, and then click **Continue** to close the **Remote Access Setup** dialog box.

    The **Windows NT Setup** dialog box appears. You will be prompted for the file location once for each protocol you configured that was not currently installed on your computer.

17. When prompted, verify the location of the files, and then click **Continue**.

    A **RIP for NWLink IPX Configuration** dialog box appears, asking if you want to enable NetBIOS broadcast propagation.

18. Click **No**.

    A **Setup Message** dialog box appears, indicating that RAS has been successfully installed.

19. Click **OK**.

    The **Network** dialog box reappears.

20. Click **Close**.

21. If your computer is running Windows NT Server, an **NWLink IPX/SPX** dialog box appears, indicating that you have multiple network adapter cards and all the internal network numbers set to 0, and offering you the chance to change them now. Click **No**.

    A **Network Setting Change** dialog box appears, asking you if you want to restart your computer now.

22. Click **Yes** to restart your computer. Be sure to start the computer as Windows NT Server or Windows NT Workstation, as appropriate.

➤ **To assign permissions to RAS users**

Note   Complete this procedure only on the computer running Windows NT Server.

---

1. Log on as Administrator.

2. Click the **Start** button, point to **Programs**, point to **Administrative Tools (Common)**, and then click **Remote Access Admin**.

    The **Remote Access Admin** dialog box appears.

3. On the **Users** menu, click **Permissions**.

    The **Remote Access Permissions** dialog box appears.

4. Click **Grant All**.

    A **Remote Access Admin** dialog box appears, requesting confirmation to grant remote access permission to all Server*x* users.

5. Click **Yes**.

    The **Remote Access Permissions** dialog box appears.

6. Click **OK**.

7. Exit Remote Access Admin.

Exercise 2
Creating a Phonebook Entry

➤   **To create a phonebook entry**

Note   Complete this exercise only on the computer running Windows NT
Workstation.

---

1. Log on to the domain as Administrator.

2. In My Computer, double-click the Dial-Up Networking icon.

    A **Dial-Up Networking** dialog box appears, stating that the phonebook
    is empty.

3. Click **OK**.

    The New Phonebook Entry wizard starts.

4. In the **Name the new phonebook entry** box, type **Server**x (where x is your
    partner's assigned student number), and then click **Next**.

    A **Server** dialog box appears.

5. Click **Next** to accept the default settings (none of the three options should
    be selected).

    A **Phone Number** dialog box appears.

6. Leave the **Phone number** blank and click **Next**.

7. Click **Finish**.

    You have just created a phonebook entry.

8. Click **Close** to exit the New Phonebook Entry wizard.

Exercise 3
Testing the RAS Installation

In this exercise, you will disconnect your computer running Windows NT Workstation from the network, and by using the RAS cable provided by your instructor, connect to your partner's computer.

If you do not have a RAS cable, do not do this exercise. Instead, complete Alternate Exercise 3, "Windows NT RAS Simulation," later in this lab.

Note Complete this exercise only on the computer running Windows NT Workstation.

➤ **To test RAS**

1. Disconnect the computer running Windows NT Workstation from the network by unplugging the network cable.

2. Using the RAS null modem cable provided by your instructor, connect your computer to your partner's computer by plugging one end into your computer's COM1 port and the other end into your partner's computer's COM1 port.

3. Shut down and restart Windows NT Workstation, selecting the **On the Network** profile.

4. Press CTRL+ALT+DELETE.

5. Click **OK** to acknowledge the logon message.

    The **Logon Information** dialog box appears.

6. Click to select the **Logon using Dial-Up Networking** check box.

7. Log on to the domain as Administrator.

    It may take a few minutes for the logon to be processed. The **Dial-Up Networking** dialog box appears.

8. In the **Phonebook entry to dial** list, click **Server***x*, and then click **Dial**.

    The **Connect to Server***x* dialog box appears.

9. In the **Password** box, type **password**

10. In the **Domain** box, type **domain**x (where x is your partner's assigned student number), and then click **OK**.

    RAS connects to the RAS server.

11. Connect to \\Instructor\Ntsrv.

12. In My Computer, double-click the Dial-Up Networking icon.

13. Click **Hang-Up**.

    A **Dial-Up Networking** dialog box appears, confirming that you want to disconnect from Server$x$.

14. Click **Yes**.

15. Click **Close**.

16. If you still have a connection to the Instructor computer, a **Dial-Up Networking** dialog box appears, trying to reconnect. Click **No, do not dial**.

Exercise 4
Removing RAS

In this exercise, you will remove RAS from your computer.

Note Complete this exercise on both computers.

➤ **To remove RAS**

1. Start the Network program.

2. Click the **Services** tab.

3. Click **Remote Access Service**.

4. Click **Remove**.

   A **Warning** dialog box appears, indicating that this action will permanently remove the component from your system, and asking if you still wish to continue.

5. Click **Yes**, and then click **Close**.

6. Remove the null-modem cable from the computers and plug the network cable into the computer that was the Dial-Up Networking client.

7. When prompted to restart your computer, click **Yes**, and then restart Windows NT Server.

Alternate Exercise 3
Windows NT RAS Simulation

In this exercise, you will use a simulation to experience how a Windows NT Dial-Up Networking client can be used to log on and connect to a computer running the Windows NT Server RAS service. In the simulation, the domain name is DOMAIN1 and the server name is Server1.

Note   Complete this exercise on your computer running Windows NT Server.

➤   **To run the RAS simulation**

1. Click the **Start** button, point to **Programs**, point to **Microsoft Windows NT 4.0 Core Technologies** Training, point to **Simulations**, and then **click RAS Simulation**.

    The simulation starts, and the **Logon Information** dialog box appears.

2. Click to select the **Logon using Dial-Up Networking** check box.

3. Verify that the domain is **DOMAIN1**.

4. Log on as Administrator using **password** as the password.

    The **Dial-Up Networking** dialog box appears.

5. Verify that the **Phonebook entry to dial** box contains **SERVER1**, and then click **Dial**.

    The **Connect to Server1** dialog box appears.

6. In the **Password** box, type **password** and then click **OK**.

    A **Connecting to Server1** dialog box appears, and RAS connects to the RAS server.

7. Double-click the Network Neighborhood icon.

8. Double-click **Server1**.

    What shares are available on Server1?

---

9. In My Computer, double-click the Dial-Up Networking icon.

10. Click **Hang-Up**.

    A **Dial-Up Networking** dialog box appears, confirming that you want to disconnect from Server1.

11. Click **Yes**, and then click **Close**.

    A **Windows NT RAS Simulation** dialog box appears.

12. Click **Exit** to close the simulation.

Lab 20: Installing Internet Information Server *(optional)*

Objectives

After completing this lab, you will be able to:

- Install Internet Installation Server (IIS).
- Identify environmental changes made to Windows NT Server 4.0 as a result of installing IIS.
- Publish documents from a newly created directory.
- Configure DNS for IIS.

Before You Begin

To complete this lab, you will need to know your assigned student number and your computer name.

Prerequisite

Lab 18: Installing and Configuring DNS.

Estimated time to complete this lab: 30 minutes

Exercise 1
Exploring the Windows NT Server Environment

In this exercise, you will explore the Windows NT Server environment before installing IIS. You will then identify the changes that installation of IIS makes to the Windows NT Server environment.

Note   Complete this exercise on your computer running Windows NT Server.

➤ **To examine the Windows NT Server environment**

1. Log on as Administrator.

2. In Control Panel, double-click the Services icon.

   The **Services** dialog box appears.

3. Scroll through the services available.

   Are there any publishing services listed? (Hint: Does the word *publishing* appear in the service name?)

   _____

4. Close the **Services** dialog box.

5. On the **Administrative Tools (Common)** menu, click **User Manager for Domains**.

6. In User Manager for Domains, examine the list of names.

   Is there an Internet Guest account listed?

   _____

7. Close User Manager for Domains.

8. On the **Administrative Tools (Common)** menu, click **Performance Monitor**.

9. In Performance Monitor, on the **Edit** menu, click **Add to Chart**.

   The **Add to Chart** dialog box appears.

10. In the **Object** box, scroll through the available objects.

    Are there any Internet-related items in the list?

    _____

11. Click **Cancel** to close the **Add to Chart** dialog box.

12. Close Performance Monitor.

Exercise 2
Installing IIS

Note Complete this exercise on your computer running Windows NT Server.

➤ **To install IIS**

1. Start the Network program.

2. Click the **Services** tab, and then click **Add**.

3. Click **Microsoft Internet Information Server 2.0**, and then click **OK**.

   The installation program prompts you for the path of the installation files.

4. Type **\\Instructor\Ntsrv** and then click **OK**.

   The **Microsoft Internet Information Server 2.0 Setup** dialog box appears.

5. Read the information in the **Microsoft Internet Information 2.0 Server Setup** dialog box, and then click **OK**.

   The following installation options appear:

   - Internet Service Manager
   - World Wide Web Service
   - WWW Service Samples
   - Internet Service Manager (HTML)
   - Gopher Service
   - FTP Service
   - ODBC Drivers and Administration

6. Select the **Internet Service Manager (HTML)** check box.

7. Verify that all options are selected, and then click **OK**.

8. Click **Yes** to create the D:\WINNT\System32\Inetsrv directory.

   The **Publishing Directories** dialog box appears, listing the default directories shown in the following table.

Directory	Path
World Wide Web Publishing Directory	D:\InetPub\wwwroot
FTP Publishing Directory	D:\InetPub\ftproot
Gopher Publishing Directory	D:\InetPub\gophroot

9. Click **OK** to accept the default directories.

10. When prompted to create the default directories, click **Yes**.

    Setup installs the IIS software.

11. When prompted to install the ODBC drivers, click **SQL Server**, and then click **OK**.

12. When Setup is complete, click **OK**.

13. Click **Close**.

Exercise 3
Identifying the Changes that Installing IIS Made to the Windows NT Server Environment

In this exercise, you will inspect the Windows NT Server environment to verify that the IIS services are installed and that an IIS Guest account exists. If you do not remember how to answer the questions, review Exercise 1.

Note Complete this exercise on your computer running Windows NT Server.

➤ **To identify changes that IIS made to the Windows NT Server environment**

1. Are any publishing services installed on your computer?

2. Are there any Internet-related user accounts on your computer?

3. Are there any Internet-related objects on your computer that Performance Monitor can monitor?

➤ **To verify that IIS is working**

1. On your desktop, double-click **Microsoft Internet Explorer**.

2. If you are not connected to the Internet, a **Microsoft Internet Explorer** dialog box appears, indicating that it could not connect to the Internet site http://www.microsoft.com. Click **OK**.

3. In Microsoft Internet Explorer, on the **File** menu, click **Open**, type your computer name, and then click **OK**.

    Does your Web server start?

4. In the **Address** box, type **ftp://**_your computer name_ and then press ENTER.

    Can you connect to your server through FTP?

5. On the **File** menu, click **Close**.

Exercise 4
Publishing Documents from a New Directory

In this exercise, you will publish a document using a directory that you create.

Note   Complete this exercise on your computer running Windows NT Server.

➤ **To publish documents from a new directory**

1. Right-click **My Computer**, and then click the Explore icon.
2. In the root of drive D, create a new folder called **NewWWW**.
3. Copy Default.htm from D:\LabFiles\Iis to D:\NewWWW.
4. Close Windows NT Explorer.
5. Click the **Start** button, point to **Programs**, point to **Microsoft Internet Server (Common)**, and then click **Internet Service Manager**.
6. On the line where **Service** is **WWW**, click **Server**x.
7. On the **Properties** menu, click **Service Properties**.
8. In the **WWW Service Properties** dialog box, click the **Directories** tab.

   What directories and aliases are listed?

   Note   If there is not enough room to see the full directory name, you can click the directory, and then click **Edit Properties** to see all of the properties for the directory, including its full directory name.

Directory	Alias

9. Click **Add**.

   The **Directory Properties** dialog box appears.
10. Click **Browse**.
11. On drive D, double-click **NewWWW**, and then click **OK**.

   The **Directory** box now contains **D:\NewWWW**.

12. Click **Virtual Directory**, and then in the **Alias** box, type **Virtual**

    This will be the published name of the new directory.

13. Click **OK** to close the **Directory Properties** dialog box.

    What directory and alias were added?

    _____

14. Click **OK** to close the **WWW Service Properties** dialog box.

15. Close Internet Service Manager.

16. Click the **Start** button, and then click **Run**.

17. In the **Open** box, type **http://Server*x*/Virtual** (where *x* is your assigned student number), and then click **OK**.

    Microsoft Internet Explorer starts, and then displays the default page in the virtual share.

18. Close Microsoft Internet Explorer.

Exercise 5
Setting Up DNS for IIS

In this exercise, you will use DNS to resolve IP addresses for IIS.

Note Complete this exercise on your computer running Windows NT Server.

➤ **To set up DNS for IIS**

1. On **Administrative Tools (Common)** menu, click **DNS Manager**.

2. Double-click your computer name.

3. In the left pane of the window that appears, double-click **corp*x*.com** (where *x* is your assigned student number).

4. In the left pane, right-click **corp*x*.com** (where *x* is your assigned student number).

5. On the menu that appears, click **New Record**.

6. Click **CNAME Record**, and then in the **Alias Name** box, type **WWW*x*** (where *x* is your assigned student number).

7. In the **For Host DNS Name** box, type **Server*x*.corp*x*.com** (where *x* is your assigned student number), and then click **OK**.

8. Verify that a resource record of type A exists for your computer. If it does not exist, create a new host resource record for your computer.

9. Close DNS Manager.

10. Start a Command Prompt.

11. At the Command Prompt, type **ping www*x*** (where *x* is your assigned student number), and then press ENTER.

   What is the name of the computer and what is the IP address?

   _____

12. Close the Command Prompt window.

13. Start Microsoft Internet Explorer.

14. In Microsoft Internet Explorer, on the **File** menu, click **Open**.

15. In the **Open** box, type **WWW*x*** (where *x* is your assigned student number), and then click **OK**.

   Does your Web server start?

   _____

16. Close Microsoft Internet Explorer.

Lab 21: Installing and Configuring GSNW

Objectives

After completing this lab, you will be able to:

- Install Gateway Services for NetWare (GSNW).
- Configure GSNW.
- Test your GSNW installation.

Before You Begin

Prerequisite

In this lab, it is assumed that the NetWare server in your classroom has been configured to allow you to log on as Administrator and be able to connect with Supervisor equivalence.

Estimated time to complete this lab: 20 minutes

Exercise 1
Installing GSNW

In this exercise, you will install GSNW.

Note Complete this exercise on your computer running Windows NT Server.

➤ **To install GSNW**

1. Start the Network program.

2. Click the **Services** tab, and then click **Add**.

   The **Select Network Services** dialog box appears.

3. Click **Gateway (and Client) Services for NetWare**, and then click **OK**.

4. When prompted for the location to copy the necessary files, type
   \\Instructor\Ntsrv and then click **Continue**.

5. Click **Close**.

   The bindings configuration, storing, and review occur, and then the **Network
   Settings Change** dialog box appears, asking you to shut down and restart
   Windows NT Server.

6. Click **Yes** to shut down, and then restart Windows NT Server.

7. When the system restarts, log on as Administrator.

   When you log on, what happens that is new?

---

8. Click **Cancel**, and then click **Yes**.

Exercise 2
Configuring GSNW

In this exercise, you will configure GSNW, which includes setting a preferred server, synchronizing your password with the Administrator password on a NetWare server, and sharing files on a NetWare server.

Note   Complete this exercise on your computer running Windows NT Server.

➤ **To configure GSNW and share files on a NetWare server**

1. In Control Panel, double-click the GSNW icon.

   The **Gateway Service for NetWare** dialog box appears.

2. In the **Select Preferred Server** list, click **NETWARE1**.

3. Click **Gateway**.

   The **Configure Gateway** dialog box appears.

4. Click to select the **Enable Gateway** check box.

5. In the **Gateway Account** box, type **Administrator**

6. In the **Password** and **Confirm password** boxes, type **password**

7. Click **Add**.

   The **New Share** dialog box appears.

8. In the **Share Name** box, type **sysvol**

9. In the **Network Path** box, type **\\netware1\sys**

10. In the **Use Drive** box, click **Z:**, and then click **OK**.

11. Click **OK** to close the **Configure Gateway** dialog box.

12. Click **OK** to close the **Gateway Service for NetWare** dialog box.

    A dialog box appears, stating that the changes will take effect the next time you log on.

13. Click **OK**.

14. Log off.

Exercise 3
Testing the GSNW Installation

In this exercise, you will check your server and those of others in your class to see that GSNW works.

Note Complete this exercise on your computer running Windows NT Server.

➤ **To check your installation**

1. Log on as Administrator.
2. Double-click **My Computer**.

   Notice that the NetWare volume is your drive Z.
3. Close My Computer.
4. At a Command Prompt, type **net share** and then press ENTER.

   Under **Share Name**, you should see **sysvol**, and under **Resource**, you should see **z:**.
5. Connect to another student's Sysvol shared volume.
6. Disconnect from all other students' Sysvol shared volumes.
7. Close the Command Prompt.

Exercise 4 *(optional)*
Configuring and Using CSNW

In this exercise, you will use a simulation to give you practice configuring and using CSNW. The simulation has you select a preferred server, and then connect to NetWare servers running bindery emulation and NDS.

Note   Complete this exercise on your computer running Windows NT Server.

➤ **To start the Novell NetWare simulation**

- Click the **Start** button, point to **Programs**, point to **Technical Support Training**, point to **Simulations**, and then click **Novell NetWare Simulation**.

  The Novell NetWare simulation begins, simulating your desktop with Control Panel open.

➤ **To select a preferred server**

1. Using the Novell NetWare simulation, in Control Panel, double-click the CSNW icon.

   The **Client Service for NetWare** dialog box appears.

2. Click **Preferred Server**.

3. In the **Select Preferred Server** list, click **CANW312DPT01**.

4. Click **OK**.

   A message box appears, indicating that your changes will take effect the next time you log on.

5. Click **OK**.

   A **Windows NT NetWare Simulation** dialog box appears, stating that the simulation will proceed as if a shutdown had occurred, and then that you restarted the computer, logging on as Administrator.

6. Click **OK**.

   A message box appears, asking you to wait while the system writes unsaved data to the disk.

   The simulation continues with Control Panel open.

➤ **To use the Syscon resource on a NetWare server running bindery emulation**

1. Using the Novell NetWare simulation, right-click **My Computer**, and then click **Map Network Drive**.

2. Double-click **CANW312DPT01**.

3. Click **SYS**, and then click **OK**.

   You are connected to the CANW312DPT01 NetWare server, with the SYS folder mapped to drive E. A window displaying the contents of the SYS folder is open on your desktop.

4. Double-click **Public**.

5. Double-click **Syscon**.

   You are now running a utility that resides on the NetWare server. For this simulation, the menu options for Syscon have been disabled.

6. To exit Syscon, press ESC, use the arrow keys to select **Yes**, and then press ENTER.

7. Right-click **My Computer**, and then click **Disconnect Network Drive**.

8. Click **CANW312DPT01\SYS**, and then click **OK**.

➤ **To select a default tree and context**

1. Using the Novell NetWare simulation, in Control Panel, double-click the CSNW icon.

   The **Client Service for NetWare** dialog box appears.

2. Click **Default Tree and Context**.

3. In the **Tree** box, type **terra_flora**

4. In the **Context** box, type **terra_flora**

5. Click **OK**.

   A message box appears, indicating that your changes will take effect the next time you log on.

6. Click **OK**.

   A **Windows NT NetWare Simulation** dialog box appears, stating that the simulation will proceed as if a shutdown had occurred, and then that you restarted the computer, logging on as Administrator.

7. Click **OK**.

   A message box appears, asking you to wait while the system writes unsaved data to the disk.

   The simulation continues with Control Panel open.

➤ **To connect to a NetWare server running NDS**

1. Using the Novell NetWare simulation, right-click **My Computer**, and then click **Map Network Drive**.

2. Double-click the Terra_flora tree.

3. Double-click the Terra_flora organization folder.

4. Click **CANW410DIV01_SYS**, and then click **OK**.

   A window appears, showing the connection to CANW410DIV01_SYS.terra_flora on the Terra_flora tree.

5. Double-click **Public**.

6. Double-click **Pconsole**.

   You are now running a utility that resides on the NetWare server. In this simulation, the menu options for Pconsole have been disabled.

7. To exit Pconsole, press ESC, use the arrow keys to select **Yes**, and then press ENTER.

8. Right-click **My Computer**, and then click **Disconnect Network Drive**.

9. Click **TERRA_FLORA\CANW410DIV01_SYS.TERRA_FLORA**, and then click **OK**.

   A **Windows NT NetWare Simulation** dialog box appears.

10. Click **Exit** to end the Novell NetWare simulation.

Lab 22: Implementing Directory Replication

Objectives

After completing this lab, you will be able to:

- Add an account for the Directory Replicator service.
- Configure the Directory Replicator service.
- Manage directory replication on a computer.
- Use the Directory Replicator service to replicate files.

Before You Begin

In this lab, you will be working with a partner. You will both complete all exercises, configuring the Directory Replicator service and replicating files from one computer to the other. Each computer will be configured as both an export server and an import computer.

To complete this lab, you will need to know your assigned student number and your partner's computer name.

Estimated time to complete this lab: 30 minutes

Exercise 1
Creating an Account for the Directory Replicator Service

In this exercise you will create an account for the Directory Replicator service to use.

Note   Complete this exercise on your computer running Windows NT Server.

➤ **To create an account for the Directory Replicator service**

1. Log on as Administrator.

2. On the **Administrative Tools (Common)** menu, click **User Manager for Domains**.

3. Create a user account by using the information in the following table.

In this field	Respond this way
Username	**repl**
Full Name	**Replicator Service Account**
Password	**password**
Confirm Password	**password**
User Must Change Password at Next Logon	Not selected
Password Never Expires	Selected
Groups	Add as a member of the Replicator group

4. Close User Manager for Domains.

Exercise 2
Configuring the Directory Replicator Service

In this exercise, you will configure the Directory Replicator service.

Note Complete this exercise on your computer running Windows NT Server.

➤ **To correct a registry entry**

1. Open Windows NT Registry Editor (Regedt32.exe).

2. On the **Options** menu, click to clear **Read Only Mode**.

3. Open the following key:

    HKEY_LOCAL_MACHINE\SYSTEM\CurrentControlSet\Control \SecurePipeServers\winreg\AllowedPaths

4. In the right pane, double-click **Machine: REG_MULTI_SZ**.

    The **Multi-String Editor** dialog box appears with four lines of data.

5. In the **Data** box, add a fifth line by pressing the DOWN ARROW key to clear the highlight, and then press ENTER.

6. Type **System\CurrentControlSet\Services\Replicator**

Caution Verify that you have added a fifth line and typed the information correctly. If you made a mistake, correct it now or click **Cancel** and begin again.

---

7. Click **OK** to close the **Multi-String Editor** dialog box.

8. Close Registry Editor.

9. Shut down and restart Windows NT Server.

10. Log on as Administrator.

➤   **To configure the Directory Replicator service**

1. In Control Panel, double-click the Services icon.

2. Click **Directory Replicator**.

3. Click **Startup**.

    A **Service** dialog box appears.

4. Under **Startup Type**, click **Automatic**.

5. Under **Log On As**, click **This Account**, and then click the ellipsis (**...**) button, located to the right of the **This Account** box.

    The **Add User** dialog box appears.

6. Click **repl**.

7. Click **Add**, and then click **OK**.

    The **Service** dialog box reappears.

8. In the **Password** and **Confirm Password** fields, type **password**

9. Click **OK**.

    A **Services** dialog box appears, stating that the repl account has been granted the Log On As A Service right.

10. Click **OK**.

11. Click **Close**.

Exercise 3
Managing Replication

In this exercise, you will manage the replication properties for the computer.

Note Complete this exercise on both computers running Windows NT Server.

➤ **To configure an export server and an import computer**

1. On the **Administrative Tools (Common)** menu, click **Server Manager**.

2. Double-click *your computer name*.

3. Click **Replication**.

   The **Directory Replication on Server**x (where *x* is your assigned student number) dialog box appears.

4. Click **Export Directories**.

5. Under **Export Directories**, click **Add**.

   The **Select Domain** dialog box appears.

6. In the **Domain** box, type *your partner's computer name* and then click **OK**.

   The **Directory Replication on Server**x (where *x* is your assigned student number) dialog box reappears.

7. Click **Import Directories**.

8. Under **Import Directories**, click **Add**.

   The **Select Domain** dialog box appears.

9. In the **Domain** box, type *your partner's computer name* and then click **OK**.

   The **Directory Replication on Server**x (where *x* is your assigned student number) dialog box reappears.

10. Click **OK**.

   Service Control Manager starts the Directory Replicator service.

Exercise 4
Replicating Files

In this exercise, you will use the Directory Replicator service to replicate some files, and then verify that replication has taken place.

Note   Complete this exercise on your computer running Windows NT Server.

➤ **To create files for replication**

1. In the D:\Winnt\System32\Repl\Export\Scripts directory, create a new folder called Profiles.

2. Copy two or three files to the Profiles folder.

➤ **To verify replication**

1. Wait approximately six minutes.

2. Verify that the files also exist in the D:\Winnt\System32\Repl\Import\Scripts directory on your partner's computer.

3. Close Server Manager.

Lab 23: Troubleshooting the Windows NT Boot Process

Objectives

After completing this lab, you will be able to:

■ Create a Windows NT boot disk for the Intel platform.

■ Invoke the Last Known Good configuration to recover from a system boot failure.

■ Identify the indications that a boot file is missing and discuss the effects of the order in which the boot files actually failed.

■ Perform an emergency repair.

Before You Begin

You will need one blank disk for creating a Windows NT boot disk (Intel platform).

The first exercise in this lab is required; the remaining exercises in this lab are optional. The remaining exercises require an additional 45 minutes to complete.

Estimated time to complete this lab: 30 minutes

Exercise 1
Creating a Windows NT Boot Disk for the Intel Platform

In this exercise, you will remove the Hidden, Read-only, and System attributes from boot files so that you can copy them. You will then create a Windows NT boot disk (for your Intel *x*86 computer) that can be used if the boot partition on your computer is not accessible.

Note Complete this exercise on your computer running Windows NT Server.

➤ **To prepare files for copying**

1. In Windows NT Explorer, click drive C.

2. On the **View** menu, click **Options**.

3. Click the **View** tab, and then click **Show All files**.

4. Click to clear the **Hide file extensions for known file types** check box, and then click **OK**.

5. Select **Boot.ini**, **Bootsect.dos**, **Ntdetect.com**, **Ntldr**, and, if it exists, **Ntbootdd.sys**.

6. On the **File** menu, click **Properties**.

7. Click to clear the **Hidden** and **Read-only** check boxes, and then click **OK**.

8. At a Command Prompt, type **attrib c:*.* -s** and then press ENTER.

   This step is necessary because Windows NT Explorer does not allow configuration of the system attributes of files and folders.

➤ **To create a Windows NT boot disk**

1. Use Windows NT Explorer to format a disk, or at a Command Prompt use the **Format.exe** command.

2. Copy the following files from the root of drive C to the root of drive A.

   - Boot.ini
   - Bootsect.dos
   - Ntdetect.com
   - Ntldr
   - Ntbootdd.sys (only if it exists)

➤ **To test the Windows NT boot disk**

1. Verify the Windows NT boot disk is in drive A.

2. Shut down, and then restart Windows NT Server.

   Were you able to successfully start your computer running Windows NT Server from the boot disk?

    YES.

3. If you were not successful, remove the disk from drive A, restart your computer, make any necessary changes to the Windows NT boot disk, and then repeat this procedure.

4. Log on as Administrator.

   Remove the Windows NT boot disk from drive A.

Exercise 2 *(optional)*
Using the Last Known Good Configuration

In this exercise, you will disable the keyboard driver and use the Last Known Good configuration to successfully reboot your computer.

Note Complete this exercise on your computer running Windows NT Server.

➤ **To disable the keyboard driver**

1. In Control Panel, double-click the Devices icon.

2. Click **i8042 Keyboard** and **PS/2 Mouse Port**, and then click **Startup**.

3. In the **Device** dialog box, click **Disabled**, and then click **OK**.

   A **Devices** dialog box appears, warning you that changing the startup type for this device may leave the system in an unusable state.

4. Click **Yes**.

5. Click **Close**.

6. Shut down, and then restart Windows NT Server.

➤ **To test the faulty configuration**

1. When the Begin Logon window appears, attempt to log on as Administrator.

   Were you successful? Why?

   YES! Keyboard was disabled

   _____

   _____

2. Use the power switch to shut off your computer.

➤ **To restore the Last Known Good configuration**

1. Restart Windows NT Server, and when the **Press spacebar now to invoke Hardware Profile/Last Known Good menu** prompt appears, press the SPACEBAR.

2. When the **Hardware Profile/Configuration Recovery Menu** appears, press L to use the Last Known Good configuration.

3. Press ENTER.

4. When the Begin Logon window appears, attempt to log on as Administrator.

   Were you successful? Why?

   yes! last good startup has been recovered

Exercise 3 *(optional)*
Identifying System File Problems

In this exercise, you will rename the system files on your hard disk to produce system boot problems. This will allow you to observe error messages for specific problems.

Note Complete this exercise on your computer running Windows NT Server.

➤ **To simulate missing files during system boot**

In this procedure, you rename four files that are used to start Windows NT. This enables you to simulate the effects of missing files, as presented in the next procedure.

1. In Windows NT Explorer, click drive C.

2. On drive C, rename each of the following files by adding a .lab extension.

    - Boot.ini
    - Bootsect.dos
    - Ntdetect.com
    - Ntldr

➤ **To observe the effect of missing system files**

In this procedure, you will observe the files in the boot sequence fail. You will see an error message that gives appropriate information about the file that failed to load. In the following table, record the error message and the file that you think has failed.

1. Shut down, and then restart the computer.

2. What error message do you see? Record your answer in the following table.

3. What file is missing? Record your answer in the following table.

4. Reboot the computer using the Windows NT boot disk, log on as Administrator, and then correct the problem by renaming the one identified file to its original name.

5. Remove the Windows NT boot disk from drive A, and then test your correction by restarting the computer.

6. If your solution is successful, the boot process will stop at the next missing file in the boot sequence. Correct this problem by repeating steps 1–5 in this procedure.

Note The last missing file requires you to choose to load MS-DOS from the **OS Loader Operating System** menu.

Error message	Missing file
Boot: Couldn't find NTLDR	
Boot: NTDETECT Failed	
ntoskrnl.sys	

7. Restart Windows NT Server.

➤ **To discuss the load order of the system files and the order in which the system files actually failed**

1. Use the results in the previous table to answer the following questions.

   What is the load order of the four system files?

   NTLDR
   NTDETECT.COM
   BOOT.INI
   BOOTSECT.

2. In what order did the four system files fail?

3. Why did Ntdetect.com fail to load second instead of Boot.ini?

Exercise 4 *(optional)*
Performing an Emergency Repair

In this exercise, you will use the Rdisk utility to update your Emergency Repair Disk. Then you will perform an emergency repair to inspect your boot sector.

Note Complete this exercise on your computer running Windows NT Server.

➤ **To update the Emergency Repair Disk**

1. Log on as Administrator.

2. Click the **Start** button, and then click **Run**.

3. Type **rdisk** and then click **OK**.

4. Click **Update Repair Info**.

   A **Repair Disk Utility** dialog box appears, stating that the repair information that was saved when you installed the system or when you last ran this utility will be deleted.

5. Click **Yes** to continue this operation.

   After the configuration is saved, a **Repair Disk Utility** dialog box appears, stating that you can create an Emergency Repair Disk that will contain a copy of the repair information in your system.

6. Click **Yes** to create an Emergency Repair Disk.

7. When prompted, insert the Emergency Repair Disk that was created during installation, and then click **OK**.

   The disk is reformatted, and then the updated repair information is copied.

8. When updating is complete, click **Exit**.

9. Remove the Emergency Repair Disk from drive A.

➤ **To use the emergency repair process**

1. Shut down, and then restart your computer by using the Windows NT Server Setup boot disk.

2. When prompted, insert Windows NT Server Setup Disk #2, and then press ENTER.

3. When the Welcome to Setup window appears, press R to initiate the Emergency Repair.

   The following options appear:

   ```
   [X] Inspect registry files
   [X] Inspect startup environment
   [X] Verify Windows NT system files
   [X] Inspect boot sector
        Continue (perform selected tasks)
   ```

4. Select the **Inspect boot sector** check box, and then clear the other check boxes.

5. Select **Continue (perform selected tasks)**, and then press ENTER.

6. Press ENTER to have Setup detect your mass storage devices.

7. When prompted, insert Windows NT Server Setup Disk #3, and then press ENTER.

8. Press ENTER to confirm the mass storage devices.

9. Press ENTER to continue the process.

10. When prompted, insert the Emergency Repair Disk into drive A, and then press ENTER.

    Setup completes the repair.

11. Remove the Emergency Repair Disk from drive A.

12. Press ENTER to restart Windows NT Server.

Lab 24: Using Diagnostic Utilities

Objectives

After completing this lab, you will be able to:

- View and control audit logs using Event Viewer.
- Filter and search for events in the event log to determine existing and potential problems.
- Use Windows NT Diagnostics (WinMSD) to view configuration information locally or on a remote computer.
- Create a report that contains a computer's configuration.
- Create a real-time Performance Monitor chart.
- Record data for analysis in a Performance Monitor log file.
- Summarize performance data in a Performance Monitor report.
- Install Network Monitor Tools and Agent.
- Use Network Monitor to capture and display network traffic.

Estimated time to complete this lab: 60 minutes

Exercise 1
Viewing Events and Controlling Audit Logs with Event Viewer

In this exercise, you will use Event Viewer to view events in the system, security, and application event logs, and to control the size of the log files.

Note Complete this exercise on your computer running Windows NT Server.

➤ **To view events**

1. Log on as Administrator.

2. Click the **Start** button, point to **Programs**, point to **Administrative Tools (Common)**, and then click **Event Viewer**.

   Event Viewer appears.

3. On the **Log** menu, click **System**.

   Different symbols precede different types of events.

4. Double-click one of each of the symbols (stop sign, exclamation point, and information symbol) one at a time to determine the type of event it represents and to see a description of the event.

   What types of events appear in your system log?

   Event log server has started.

   Could not locate the device of

5. On the **Log** menu, click **Security**.

   What types of events appear in your security log?

   _____

   _____

6. On the **Log** menu, click **Application**.

   What types of events appear in your Application log?

   _____

   _____

➤   **To control the size and contents of a log file**

  1. In Event Viewer, on the **Log** menu, click **Log Settings**.

      By default, what is the maximum log size for the system, security, and application log files?

      _512K_

  2. In the **Change Settings for** list, click **System**.

  3. Click **Overwrite Events As Needed**.

      How will this setting affect the system log?

      when the 512K max space is exceeded

  4. Click **OK**.   _it will overwrite_

Exercise 2
Filtering and Searching for Events

In this exercise, you will use Event Viewer to filter events and search for specific events to locate existing and potential problems.

Note Complete this exercise on your computer running Windows NT Server.

➤ **To filter events**

1. In Event Viewer, on the **Log** menu, click **Open**.
2. In the D:\LabFiles\Events folder, double-click **Sample1.evt**.

   The **Open File Type** dialog box appears.
3. Click **System**, and then click **OK**.
4. On the **View** menu, click **Filter Events**.
5. In the **Source** list, click **Nbf**, and then click **OK**.
6. Double-click the oldest entry.

   What is the description of the problem?

   _____

   What do you think is the actual problem?

   _____

7. Click **Close** to close the event and return to the log.

➤   **To search for specific messages**

1. On the **Log** menu, click **Open**.

2. Open D:\LabFiles\Events\Sample2.evt as a system log.

3. On the **View** menu, click **Filter Events**.

4. In the **Types** box, make sure that only the **Warning** check box is selected, and then click **OK**.

5. Double-click the first entry.

   What is the description of the problem?

   _____

   What action is necessary?

   _____

6. Click **Close**.

7. On the **View** menu, click **Filter Events**.

8. Under **Types**, click to select the **Error** check box, click to clear the **Warning** check box, and then click **OK**.

9. Click each entry and view its description one at a time until you determine what the problem is.

   What is the problem?

   _____

   What action is necessary?

   _____

10. Close Event Viewer.

Exercise 3
Using Windows NT Diagnostics to View Configuration Information

In this exercise, you will use WinMSD to view configuration information both locally and on a remote computer.

Note Complete this exercise on your computer running Windows NT Server.

➤ **To view software configuration information**

1. Click the **Start** button, point to **Programs**, point to **Administrative Tools (Common)**, and then click **Windows NT Diagnostics**.

2. Locate the following information by reviewing the tabs in the Windows NT Diagnostics window. In the following table, record the name of the tab and the value for the requested information.

Requested information	Tab	Value
Registered owner	*Version*	*server 09*
Registered organization	*"*	*CLU.*
Version number	*"*	
Build number	*"*	*1981, Service Pack 1*
System root (windir)		
Domain name		
CPU type		

3. Locate the following information, and then record the value of the requested information.

Requested information	Your configuration
Total physical memory	
Available physical memory	
Total page file space	
Available page file space	
Paging files	

4. List the service dependencies for the following services. (Hint: Click the
   Services tab, click the name of the service, and then click **Properties**.)

Service	Dependencies
ClipBook Server	
Network DDE	
Network DDE DSDM	
Server	
Messenger	

5. List the services that are currently running on your server.

➣ **To view configuration information for \\Instructor**

1. On the **File** menu, click **Select Computer**.

   The **Select Computer** dialog box appears.

2. In the **Computer** box, type **Instructor** and then click **OK**.

   What tabs are available for remote computers?

   Version, System, Display, Services, Resources, Environment, Network

3. Locate the following information about \\Instructor.

Requested information	\\Instructor configuration
CPU type	
Network adapter IRQ	
Video driver in use	
Domain name	

Exercise 4
Saving a Windows NT Diagnostics Report

In this exercise, you will save a Windows NT Diagnostics report for \\Instructor, and then view the report.

Note Complete this exercise on your computer running Windows NT Server, with Windows NT Diagnostics active and focused on \\Instructor.

➤ **To create a Windows NT Diagnostics report for \\Instructor**

1. On the **File** menu, click **Save Report**.

   The **Create Report** dialog box appears.

2. Under **Scope**, click **All Tabs**.

3. Under **Detail Level**, click **Complete**.

4. Click **OK**.

   The **Save WinMSD Report** dialog box appears.

5. Save the file as **C:\Msdrpt.txt**.

   The **Generating WinMSD Report** dialog box appears, containing a status bar indicating the current progress.

6. Click **OK** to exit Windows NT Diagnostics.

➤ **To read a Windows NT Diagnostics report**

1. Start Windows NT Explorer, and then click drive C.

2. Double-click **Msdrpt.txt** to view your report.

   Notepad starts, and then displays the Msdrpt.txt file.

3. On the **Search** menu, click **Find**, and then locate the following information in Msdrpt.txt.

Requested information	\\Instructor configuration
PROCESSOR_ARCHITECTURE	*x86*
PROCESSOR_LEVEL	*6*
PROCESSOR_IDENTIFIER	*x86 Family 6 Model 5 Stepping 2*
PROCESSOR_REVISION	*C502* *Genuine*

4. Close Notepad, and then close Windows NT Explorer.

Exercise 5
Creating a Real-Time Performance Monitor Chart

In this exercise, you will create a chart in Performance Monitor to display performance data in real time. Real-time charts provide a quick overview of the current performance of your system.

Note Complete this exercise on your computer running Windows NT Server.

➤ **To configure the chart**

1. Click the Start button, point to Programs, point to Administrative Tools (Common), and then click Performance Monitor.

2. On the **View** menu, click **Chart**.

3. On the **Edit** menu, click **Add To Chart**.

   Notice that **Processor** is the default object.

4. In the **Counter** list, click **%DPC Time**, and then click **Explain**.

   Notice that the **Counter Definition** appears at the bottom of the window.

5. Click each of the counters for the **Processor** object and read the **Counter Definition** for each.

6. In the **Counter** box, select all the counters available for **Processor**, and then click **Add**.

7. Click **Done**.

   A graph appears, displaying the real-time activities for the processor.

➤   **To generate data and view it on the chart**

1. Click the **Start** button, point to **Programs**, point to **Accessories**, point to **Games**, and then click **Pinball**.

2. Play one ball (and *only* one ball) of Pinball.

3. Close Pinball, and then switch to Performance Monitor.

4. In the list of counters, click **% Processor Time**, and notice the changing **Average** value.

Tip   To highlight the selected counter, press CTRL+H

---

5. Minimize Performance Monitor.

6. Start and minimize both Server Manager and Disk Administrator.

7. Close both Server Manager and Disk Administrator.

8. Restore Performance Monitor.

9. Notice the activity on the chart, such as spikes.

You have now created a chart displaying real-time processor utilization. This is useful to see how your CPU is being used at the current time. In the next exercise, you will collect and save data for future reference, which can then be turned into a graph to compare with real-time data to analyze performance.

Exercise 6
Recording Data for Analysis in a Performance Monitor Log File

In this exercise, you will use Performance Monitor to create and view a log of processor activity. Logs gather and record data to a file over a period of time. Logs are useful in predicting long-term trends or in troubleshooting short-term problems.

Note Complete this exercise on your computer running Windows NT Server.

➤ **To create a log**

1. In Performance Monitor, on the **View** menu, click **Log**.
2. On the **Edit** menu, click **Add To Log**.
3. In the **Objects** list, click **Processor**, and then click **Add**.

Note When you select an object for a log, all counters for that object will be recorded in the log automatically.

---

4. Click **Done**.
5. On the **Options** menu, click **Log**.
6. In the **File Name** box, type in a name for the log, using your name and a .log extension.

   For example, if your name is Abigail, name your log file Abigail.log.
7. Under **Update Time**, set **Periodic Update Interval** to **1** second.
8. Click **Start Log**.

   The Log window appears, with real-time processor activity being collected in the log.
9. Create processor activity by starting applications or moving the mouse.
10. In Performance Monitor, periodically check the **File Size** box to determine the size of your data file.
11. Wait until the file has reached 100 KB, and then proceed with the next step.
12. On the **Options** menu, click **Log**, and then click **Stop Log**.

➤   **To view log data in a chart**

1. On the **View** menu, click **Chart**.

2. On the **Options** menu, click **Data From**.

3. Click **Log File**, and then click the ellipsis (**...**) button.

4. Click the log file that you just created, and then click **Open**.

5. Click **OK** to return to Performance Monitor.

    An empty Chart window appears.

6. On the **Edit** menu, click **Add To Chart**.

7. Select all counters available for **Processor**, and then click **Add**.

8. Click **Done**.

The chart displays the processor counters collected in your log during the log collection period. You will notice data displayed on the chart as well as on the status bar. The **Last**, **Average**, **Minimum**, and **Maximum** values are displayed with the total graph time from your log of data.

Exercise 7
Summarizing Performance Data in a Performance Monitor Report

In this exercise, you will view portions of the data in a chart to isolate specific information. You will also use reports to view data in a nongraphical format.

Note   Complete this exercise on your computer running Windows NT Server.

➤ **To view isolated segments of log data in a chart**

1. In the list of counters, click **% Processor Time**.

2. Using information from the status bar, record the value for **Average of % Processor Time**.

---

3. On the **Edit** menu, click **Time Window**.

   The **Input Log File Timeframe** dialog box appears. This dialog box contains a slider that is used to adjust the portion of the chart that is shown in Performance Monitor. By default, the entire chart is shown.

Note   You may need to move the Input Log File Timeframe window to see the entire chart.

---

4. Click the left section of the slider, drag this section to the middle of the bar, and then click **OK**.

   The right half of the original chart is now displayed in Performance Monitor.

5. Record the value for **Average of % Processor Time** again.

---

6. Repeat steps 3 and 4, this time adjusting the slider so that the last one-quarter of the chart is displayed.

7. Record the value for **Average of % Processor Time** again.

---

8. Repeat steps 3 and 4, adjusting the left and right sections of the sliding bar as necessary, until the **Average of % Processor Time** for the portion of the chart displayed in Performance Monitor is greater than 40 percent.

   In your opinion, how accurate is this representation of the processor's use?

---

9. Edit the Time window to view the entire graph.

➤   **To create a report showing the % Processor Time for the entire graph period**

1. On the **View** menu, click **Report**.

   A blank Report window appears.

2. On the **Edit** menu, click **Add To Report**.

3. With **Processor** as the default object, in the **Counter** list, select all counters, and then click **Add**.

4. Click **Done**.

   A report with the chosen counters is displayed, showing the averages.

5. What was the average **% Processor Time** for the entire graph period?

   _____

6. Close Performance Monitor.

Exercise 8
Installing Network Monitor Tools and Agent

In this exercise, you will install Network Monitor Tools and Agent.

Note   Complete this exercise on your computer running Windows NT Server.

➤   **To install Network Monitor Tools and Agent**

1. Start the Network program.

2. Click the **Services** tab.

3. Click **Add**.

4. In the **Network Service** box, click **Network Monitor Tools and Agent**, and then click **OK**.

5. In the **Windows NT Setup** dialog box, type **\\instructor\ntsrv** and then click **Continue**.

   Windows NT Setup copies the required files.

6. After the files have been copied, click **Close**.

7. When prompted, click **Yes** to shut down and restart Windows NT Server.

Exercise 9
Capturing Data with Network Monitor

In this exercise, you will use Network Monitor to capture and display network traffic.

Note   Complete this exercise on your computer running Windows NT Server.

➤ **To set a trigger**

1. Log on as Administrator.

2. Click the **Start** button, point to **Programs**, point to **Administrative Tools (Common)**, and then click **Network Monitor**.

   The Network Monitor Capture window appears.

3. On the **Capture** menu, click **Trigger**.

   The **Capture Trigger** dialog box appears.

4. Under **Trigger on**, click **Buffer Space**.

5. Under **Buffer Space**, click **50%**.

6. Under **Trigger Action**, click **Stop Capture**, and then click **OK**.

➤ **To capture network data and generate network traffic**

1. On the **Capture** menu, click **Start**.

2. On your desktop, click the **Start** button, and then click **Run**.

3. In the **Open** box, type **\\instructor** and then click **OK**.

   A list of resources on \\Instructor appears.

4. In the Instructor window, double-click **Ntsrv**.

➤ **To view network data statistics**

1. Switch to Network Monitor.

2. On the **Capture** menu, click **Stop**.

3. On the **Capture** menu, click **Display Captured Data**.

4. Scroll through the list of captured frames. You should see your own computer name (**Server**x) and **Instructor**. You may also see other computer names if those computers were communicating with your server during the capture.

5. Close Network Monitor.

6. Close both the Ntsrv on Instructor and Instructor windows.